Original title:
The Poetry of Christmas Mornings

Copyright © 2024 Creative Arts Management OÜ
All rights reserved.

Author: Rosalie Bradford
ISBN HARDBACK: 978-9916-90-938-6
ISBN PAPERBACK: 978-9916-90-939-3

Swirling Snowflakes of Joy

Swirling snowflakes dance in the air,
Hitting my nose with a ticklish flair.
I catch one on my tongue with a grin,
But it melts away before I begin.

Kids in the park are building a beast,
A snowman with a carrot for a feast.
Its eyes made of rocks and a scarf too tight,
Looks more like a snow blob than a sight.

Snowball fights erupt, oh what a scene!
I wind up hit—by a snowball machine.
Laughter erupts amidst the white haze,
Who knew frozen fluff could bring such glows?

As I trip and tumble in snowdrifts so deep,
I think of the winter, a funny old leap.
With each chilly gust that makes me a shiver,
I can't help but laugh—December's a giver!

The Magic of Morning Light

The sun peeks in, a sleepy grin,
Coffee brews, let the day begin.
Socks mismatched, a fashion spree,
Chasing my cat, oh, where could she be?

Toaster pops, with a crispy cheer,
Toast flies high, giving a little fear.
Butter slips, like a smooth ballet,
Morning chaos, but hey, that's okay!

A Whispering Winter Wonderland

Snowflakes dance, oh what a sight,
Falling fast, like a feathered flight.
Building snowmen, not quite so tall,
Till they topple, laughing, we all fall.

Hot cocoa spills, on my brand new hat,
Sipping slow, while I pet the cat.
Snowball fights turn into a race,
And I lose track of my own face!

Echoes of Laughter in the Air

Children play, their giggles ring,
Chasing shadows, like a spring fling.
Their laughter echoes, a joyful sound,
Bouncing high, as they twirl around.

Tickle fights in the living room,
Laughter bursts, like a bright balloon.
Silly jokes, and wide-eyed stares,
Creating memories in small cuddly pairs.

The Promise of a New Day

Alarm clocks buzz, not a gentle sound,
Each snooze a battle, but sleep is profound.
Yet here comes breakfast, hot and bright,
Pancakes stack high, a happy sight.

Plans unfold with a hopeful glee,
With every step, we find the key.
Embrace the day, let dreams take flight,
In the dance of morning, everything feels right.

Echoing Laughter in the Cold

In winter's chill, we laugh out loud,
Sipping hot cocoa, feeling proud.
Snowmen wink with a carrot grin,
As frostbite waits for us to win.

We slip on ice, a comical sight,
Flailing like fish in a snowy fight.
The dog spins round, so full of glee,
Chasing snowflakes, oh how carefree!

Our cheeks are red, our noses too,
Wrapped in scarves, a colorful view.
We sing off-key, a chorus grand,
'Til frozen fingers halt our band.

Through chilly air, our giggles soar,
Joyful voices, we can't ignore.
In winter's grasp, we find our cheer,
Echoing laughter, loud and clear.

Kindled Hearts in the Morning Light

The sun peeks in, to start the day,
With coffee brewed in a funny way.
Socks mismatched, oh what a sight,
Yet hearts are warm, and spirits bright.

Toast pops up like a happy jig,
Butter melting on a golden twig.
Jam splatters, it's quite the scene,
Starting mornings like a dream routine.

We dance around in our pajamas,
Laughing at silly old dramas.
Morning light reveals our cheer,
Kindled hearts, banishing fear.

With laughter loud and smiles wide,
We greet the day with joyful stride.
Each moment shared is pure delight,
In these simple joys, our hearts take flight.

A Symphony of Winter Whimsy

Snowflakes fall like playful tunes,
Dancing under the watchful moons.
Skiing down hills with joyful shouts,
We tumble and roll, despite our doubts.

Fireside tales with marshmallows golden,
Hot chocolate spills, the laughter's beholden.
The cat dons a hat, oh what a sight,
Purring along, it's quite the delight.

Chilled fingers toast by the crackling flame,
Each silly slip, a victorious claim.
Frosty breath makes funny shapes,
In our winter wonderland, laughter escapes.

Snowball fights, with giggles so clear,
The joy of winter's harmonizing cheer.
In this symphony, we find our play,
Whimsy alive in the cold, every day.

Gifts of Love in Every Moment

A gift of laughter, wrapped with glee,
A wink from you, just because, you see.
The socks you bought, in colors bright,
They mismatch still, yet feel so right.

Each moment shared like a cozy prize,
In silly faces or sweet surprise.
A heart-shaped cookie with frosting galore,
We savor each bite, then ask for more.

In all we do, love's sparkling light,
Turns mundane tasks into sheer delight.
With goofy gifs and warm embraces,
These gifts of love, time never erases.

So here's to moments, big and small,
With laughter echoing, we cherish it all.
In every glance, every silly jest,
Love is the gift, we find the best.

The Light of Family Gatherings

A table filled with dishes grand,
Uncle Joe takes the last green band.
A toast to good times, spilled on the floor,
And Aunt May's casserole that we all ignore.

The kids run wild like cats on a spree,
Grandma's yelling, 'Not near the tree!'
Cousins trading secrets and candy galore,
While Dad's cooking burgers we can't really score.

Laughter erupts, it all feels just right,
Till the dog snatches a bun in full flight.
We all gather close, with hearts filled with cheer,
As mom shouts, 'Dinner!' we all start to steer.

Heartfelt Moments Wrapped in Time

A photo so flawed of our family style,
Dad with a grin, and he's lost his dial.
Mom sneezes so loud, we've captured the scene,
But Aunt Edna's wig? Oh, that's just obscene!

We gather together in mismatched socks,
With stories of turkeys that came with a box.
Dad's tripping over the cat once again,
While laughter erupts like it's just pure zen.

Every moment a treasure, in frames they remain,
So we throw out the bad ones and keep all the sane.
Wrapped in our memories, oh what a sight,
These heartfelt moments, forever polite.

Frosty Fingers and Warm Hearts

Outside it's chilly, winter's a beast,
Inside we're cozy, it's hot chocolate feast.
With marshmallows floating and laughter so bright,
We huddle together, everything's right.

Snowflakes are falling, we're all bundled tight,
But Uncle Bob struggles—a snowman in sight.
His nose is a carrot, oh what a mess,
Snowballs a-flying, he really won't guess.

We shake off the cold with hot cocoa vibes,
Building our dreams in our own winter jibes.
Frosty fingers hold warm hands with glee,
In this chilly season, our hearts dance so free.

Morning Kisses of Flurry

Alarm clocks chirping like birds in a race,
Coffee's the prize, we all crave that taste.
Mornings with kids are a delightful zoo,
'Where's my shoe?' 'Did you eat my goo?'

Pajamas are worn, with mismatched flair,
Everyone's buzzing like they just don't care.
A race to the kitchen, who's first for the jam?
In the middle of chaos, I hug the whole fam.

Snow's on the ground, a wintery glow,
Kisses fulfilled in a flurry of snow.
We dive into the day with giggles and cheer,
For every new morning brings loved ones so near.

The Magic of Wrapped Surprises

A box with a bow, oh what could it be?
A sock with a hole? A rubber chicken, maybe?
It's wrapped up so tight, I can hardly guess,
Unraveling laughter, what a fun mess!

Each layer I peel, the suspense grows steep,
A gift from my aunt, who's just lost her sheep.
Inside there's a sweater, too snug for my frame,
But I'll wear it with pride, oh what a wild game!

There's something about gifts that defy all sense,
Like a fruitcake that lands with a thud and suspense.
So here's to the joy in surprises we find,
Especially the ones that are totally blind!

Wrapped up in laughter, that's how we'll cheer,
With each silly gift that brings giggles near.
So next time you gift, just remember the laughs,
The magic of timing, and quirky gaffs!

Gentle Chimes in the Winter Sky

The snowflakes dance, like tweets in the breeze,
A wintery choir, bringing chills to our knees.
As chimes start to tinkle, my teeth start to chatter,
Is that more cold air, or just heated small talk matter?

Hot cocoa in hand, I sip with a grin,
While snowmen gossip about the hats they win.
I swear I just heard a jingle and chime,
Or perhaps it's old Bob, still singing out of time.

Icicles dangle with a glint in their eye,
Are they plotting a coup or just living to try?
Each flake is a joke, though they melt away fast,
Their laughter is fleeting, yet completely steadfast.

So let's raise a cup to the winter's cool charms,
While we snuggle together, all wrapped in warm arms.
With chimes in the distance, we'll dance through the night,
And forget all our worries, in this chilly delight!

A Quilt of Warmth and Wonder

A patchwork of colors, sewn by our dreams,
Each square tells a story and whispers of schemes.
With laughter and love stitched into the seam,
This quilt of warmth makes every heart beam.

On cold winter nights, it's the ultimate hug,
A fortress of fabric, all cozy and snug.
It's like grandma's secret, a sprinkle of glee,
This blanket of joy wraps enchantments in spree.

Spilled popcorn and soda make the best stains,
As we watch cheesy movies, endearing their gains.
With each gentle tug, we share tales anew,
Of monsters and myths, and magic that flew.

So gather around, the night's still so young,
With a quilt full of wonder, our laughter is sung.
Embrace the connection, the warmth we all know,
In patches of happiness, together we glow!

Northern Lights and Candlelight

The sky is a painter, in green, pink, and gold,
With colors that shimmer, a sight to behold.
Wrapped up in blankets, we'll gaze, wide-eyed,
As the lights dance above, like a glorious tide.

With candles aglow, we banish the chill,
Each flicker a giggle, each shadow a thrill.
The world feels like magic, as stars play peek-a-boo,
While we roast marshmallows, and make s'mores for the crew.

"Oh look, there's a moose!" someone shouts with delight,
As it tiptoes away, into the soft night.
With laughter we share, by the warm candle's glow,
These moments remind us, just how love can grow.

So here's to the nights of the northern embrace,
Where the lights weave our dreams in a shimmering lace.
With each giggle and chuckle, let time hold us tight,
In a tapestry woven of sparkle and light!

Whispers of Frosted Dawn

The alarm clock clinks, it's time to rise,
Yet frostbitten toes just try to disguise.
The coffee pot hisses, a bubbling mess,
As I dance in my robe, quite the morning stress.

The cat claims the sunbeam, a royal decree,
While I'm left in shadows, just sipping my tea.
The toast jumps around, it's more like a race,
I wonder if mornings are a cruel, cruel face.

Snowflakes are plotting a soft little prank,
As I slip on the ice, nearly walk off the plank.
Yet laughter erupts through the frosty air,
Mornings like this mean I'm free as a sparrow's dare.

So here's to the dawn with its frosty embrace,
Where giggles can tumble and smiles find their place.
Embrace every slip, every fall, every fawn,
In the whimsical whispers of frosted dawn.

Echoes of Joyful Laughter

In the kitchen, cookies are clearly a feat,
As flour clouds form and choco chips greet.
Mom's making faces, the taste test is here,
It's a holiday mystery—what will appear?

The dog is a thief, he's plotting away,
Sneaking a cookie as children play.
Joyful giggles and crumbs all around,
Laughter erupts, what wonders are found!

The tree's tipped over, oh what a mess,
Ornaments laughing, they clearly digress.
Sibling talents show, a song they will croon,
As Dad twirls around, the mad disco tune.

So raise up your cookies and dance through the night,
With echoes of laughter, everything's right.
For joy is a whisper that twinkles and teeters,
In the whole house, good humor's the meter.

Candles in the Winter Glow

Candles flicker brightly, a dance on the shelf,
They whisper sweet secrets like no one but self.
The cat pawed the table, a general glee,
Offering chaos, as only cats see.

Hot cocoa's on standby, a marshmallow fight,
With sprinkles and giggles making it bright.
Someone's a barista with whipped cream like snow,
With each silly sip, they feel pure winter glow.

The fireplace crackles, a warm cozy nook,
Where stories unfold in the family book.
Grandpa's tall tales mingle with laughter, you know,
As shadows create shapes that shuffle and flow.

So light up the candles, let laughter ignite,
In the winter wonder where hearts feel so light.
With dreams weaving stories and spirits that soar,
In the warmth of the glow, we always want more.

Wrapped in Tinsel Dreams

The tree's got bling, it's wrapped head to toe,
With tinsel so shiny, it loves to showboat.
A squirrel peeks in, it's planning a scheme,
To swipe some bright baubles in rolled-up sweet dreams.

Socks hang with joy, all mismatched and proud,
They giggle in clusters—they can't quite be loud.
Every odd sock from the corner, so bright,
Is wrapped in the magic of the seasonal night.

The gingerbread army stands brave on the tray,
With candy cane weapons defending the way.
But frosting attacks and a kid, oh so sly,
Devours their sweetness with gusto, oh my!

So here's to the tinsel, the laughter, the cream,
The holidays dance in a whimsical dream.
With every bright shimmer, let joy take its flight,
And wrap all our wishes in pure, twinkling light.

Cherished Traditions Unfold

Every year we bake the pies,
But oh, the flour often flies.
The cat now wears a festive hat,
It thinks it's just a party brat.

Uncle Joe has done it again,
He's wrapped a gift in his old pen.
We laugh so hard, we might just fall,
Family chaos, we embrace it all.

Grandma's tales are never short,
Of luck and love she will consort.
We gather 'round, the stories flow,
Who knew the past was quite this slow?

With secret Santa mischief rife,
It's thrilling in our family life.
Traditions old will never fade,
In humor's light, they're lovingly displayed.

The Spirit Within Each Stocking

We hang our stockings with great cheer,
Filled with candy, toys, and beer.
But socks have gone on quite a spree,
Now dance around the old pine tree.

Each one's stuffed with mystery treats,
The dog has claimed the ones he meets.
A squeaky toy and a random shoe,
'Twas not my choice, I swear it's true!

As morning comes, we gather round,
And what we find is tightly bound.
A mix of goodies, odd and strange,
A year's supply of Christmas change!

So cheers to stockings, odd and bright,
They hold our laughter, pure delight.
Each year we hope and laugh and sigh,
For all the joyful things we buy!

Splendour of a Starlit Night

The stars above, they twinkle bright,
As we stroll home in pure delight.
But tripping on my own two feet,
I tumble into snow, so sweet!

The moon is full, it lights the way,
We sing off-key, but who can say?
A raccoon joins our festive song,
Dance with us, we'll all sing along!

I lost my mittens in the fray,
The cold, it bites, but hey, hooray!
With snowflakes sticking on our nose,
We seek out marshmallows for our woes.

So here's to nights of icy fun,
Where laughter glows like rays from the sun.
In the splendour of the winter's call,
We find our joy, we find it all!

Laughter Beneath the Boughs

Beneath the tree, we sit and share,
With silly hats and festive wear.
A jingle bell gets stuck in hair,
Laughter erupts, we all declare!

The cookies bake, and oh, what smell,
I've burnt some too, but who can tell?
With crumbs like snowflakes on the floor,
We won't stop munching, we want more!

The presents pile in a big old heap,
While all the kiddos run and leap.
In wrapping paper, they get lost,
And scream with joy, at any cost.

So here's to joy, to merry cheer,
To family love, we hold so dear.
With laughter ringing through the pines,
It's these sweet moments that truly shine!

A Carousel of Cheer

Round and round we go, so bright,
With horses that take flight at night.
Grab your hat and hold on tight,
For giggles are our ticket flight.

The merry-go-round spins with glee,
While popcorn flies from kids in spree.
Count the ducks and make a plea,
To ride again – oh, won't it be free!

Clowns juggle pies and pies of clowns,
While laughter echoes all through town.
In this fun fair, we wear no frowns,
Just silly hats and silly crowns.

So join the ride, let joy be clear,
With friends and laughter, spread the cheer!
A carousel spins, our hearts, it steers,
In this whimsical world, we're pioneers!

Fragrant Pines and Fond Anticipations

In the woods, the pine trees sway,
As squirrels frolic and bounce, hooray!
They gather nuts in a silly play,
While birds sing songs to start the day.

The air smells sweet, like grandma's pie,
With promises of laughter, oh so spry.
Anticipation fills the sky,
Like a kite ready for a joyful fly.

We chase the shadows and dance on leaves,
In a world where nothing deceives.
Beneath the pines, nothing achieves
More joy than that which nature weaves.

So grab your friend, let's run and dive,
Through fragrant pines where we feel alive.
In this grand world, together we thrive,
And the laughter sings, we truly jive!

Frosted Wishes on the Air

Snowflakes tumble, oh what a sight,
Frosted wishes in pure delight.
Bundles of giggles take to flight,
With snowmen dancing, oh so bright!

Hot cocoa spills, a little bit sweet,
While mittens and socks lose their heat.
Snowball fights turn silly, not discreet,
As we trip and fall, nothing's complete!

Cheers echo through the snowy peaks,
While rosy cheeks share joyful streaks.
In a wonderland, it's laughter that speaks,
Beneath the sky, where all feel unique.

Frosted wishes float on the breeze,
With every slide, it's belly laughs that tease.
In this wintry world, let's find our ease,
And make snow angels that never freeze!

Boughs of Joy and Laughter

Under the branches, we gather round,
With snacks and stories that know no bound.
Giggles echo in this joyful sound,
As we dance in circles, feeling profound.

The boughs are heavy with dreams and cheer,
Decorated with smiles and holiday gear.
Laughter flies high, without any fear,
As friends and family draw near.

Silly hats and reindeer games,
With playful tricks and funny names.
In this moment, nothing's the same,
As joy ignites like warming flames.

So let's twirl beneath the sky so bright,
With boughs of joy and hearts alight.
In unity, we soar to new heights,
For love and laughter make ours a happy plight!

Reflections of Joy Beneath the Tree

Squirrels dance in a silly way,
Each leaps over a branch, hooray!
Wrapped in ribbons, gifts galore,
I think I saw a cat explore!

Laughter bubbles like a stream,
All around it feels like a dream.
With twinkling lights, we'll sing no fear,
Let's toast marshmallows, my dear!

Cookie crumbs on the carpet spread,
Everywhere they are, instead!
Santa's sleigh needs a good tune-up,
Oh dear, hope it's not a hiccup!

Underneath the branches wide,
A surprise party we'll not hide.
Beneath the tree, let's count the glee,
With giggles, hugs, and a cheeky breeze!

A Cup of Cheer on the Table

Hot cocoa spills on my new shirt,
The marshmallows are caught in the dirt!
With laughter rising in the air,
I wonder if that's a cookie stare?

Muffin hats for my dear old cat,
He looks confused, imagine that!
Cupfuls of cheer are everywhere,
A dance-off challenge? Oh, beware!

We sip from mugs, with eyes so wide,
Wondering where all the sprinkles hide.
A gust of wind bursts through the door,
And cake pops roll across the floor!

So gather 'round, my merry friends,
Let's toast to cheer that never ends.
A cup of joy, let's make a pact,
To keep the giggling, that's a fact!

Frosty Breath and Cozy Embrace

The air is crisp, I see my breath,
A chilly scene, but filled with zest.
Snowflakes tumble, a merry chase,
As I trip on a playful face!

Bundle up in scarves so bright,
Fuzzy socks, what a sight!
A snowman friend, with a pie for a hat,
Don't be shy, come join the chat!

Hot soup brews in a silly pot,
It sings a tune that hits the spot.
We chuckle at the frosty spree,
With snowballs flying, oh let it be!

Cozy whispers by the flame,
"Forget the cold, let's play a game!"
Frosty breath and warm embrace,
Winter fun, a joyful place!

Jingle Joys at Dawn

Whispers of jingle bells ignite,
The morning sun feels just right.
With sleepy heads and dreams so wry,
We dance like penguins, oh me, oh my!

Pancakes stack so high, can't wait,
Maple syrup? What a fate!
We giggle loud with every flip,
Who knew breakfast could be a trip?

Elves in pajamas join the fun,
We all agree, let's not outrun!
Pillow fights and chocolate spree,
Who knew mornings could be so free?

So here's to dawn with cheer and light,
May laughter guide us day and night.
With jingle joys, let's toast and yawn,
To every silly, lovely dawn!

Cherished Moments in Soft Footsteps

In slippers worn, I roam the house,
Chasing crumbs with my tiny mouse.
Yet every step's a grand ballet,
As I tiptoe past the pets at play.

Moments shared with donuts and tea,
A pajama party—just my cat and me.
We giggle softly at the news,
While twirling in our polka-dot shoes.

Each mischief's often a glorious tale,
As I trip on socks, and suddenly pale.
But laughter spills like jelly on toast,
In soft footsteps, I cherish the most.

So here's to slippers, and fun-filled nights,
And cats who love their cozy sights.
A life that's silly, in every way,
In cherished moments, I long to stay.

A Tincture of Spruce and Spice

I brewed a tea of spruce and spice,
It tasted odd, not very nice.
I whispered to the pot, 'Not fair!'
It simmered back with my frothy hair.

Pumpkin pie with a twisty zest,
An accidental cooking contest!
The cookies burned, the cake did flop,
But oh, the laughter would never stop.

I sprinkled cloves like fairy dust,
But all I brewed was utter rust.
Still, I serve it with a wink and grin,
For warmth and humor are the best win.

So gather 'round, you friends of grace,
Let's sip this mess with silly face.
A tincture of bliss on a chilly night,
With spice and laughter, everything's bright.

Dancing Shadows of the Festive Day

Beneath the lights, the shadows prance,
As I trip on my own two feet, a clumsy dance.
With every twirl, the cookies start to shake,
And all the lights waver, for goodness sake!

The cat joins in, a furry delight,
Leaping through shadows, giving quite a fright.
We swirl through the night, a joyous crew,
As the punch bowl spills, in glittery blue.

Neighbors poke heads, curious and bold,
"What's happening here?" they shyly behold.
Then laughter erupts, a hilarious display,
As we dance like fools on this festive day.

So let's raise a glass to the wild and bright,
To dancing shadows that fill the night.
In our playful mischief, we find our way,
To cherish each moment, this festive day.

Silent Night's Last Breath

In the quiet hush, I hear a snore,
'Twas Santa's last breath, now I'm not sure.
But is it jolly? Or is it just me?
Drifting off with sugarplum glee?

The cookies gone, a crime on the floor,
I tiptoe softly, but my nose does implore.
Was that a sleigh? Or just my old van?
The night is silent, like a snoozing man.

Yet in the stillness, I spy a light,
A glow from the tree, oh what a sight!
But is it magic, or my cat's shiny eye?
Both lead me to wonder, as I sigh.

So I whisper wishes, while snoozing in tight,
For silent night's breath, as dreams take flight.
In a world so cheeky, let laughter unfurl,
And may all our dreams create a twinkling swirl.

Glistening Dreams Unfolding

In my dream, I sprouted wings,
But made a mess of all the things.
I crashed into a pie-filled sky,
Now I can't stop eating—oh my!

Chased a rainbow, slipped in mud,
Landed hard with quite a thud.
Where's my pot of gold, I ask,
Instead, I'm stuck with this weird task!

Dancing squirrels in tutus prance,
Thought I saw them take a chance.
But they just launched a nutty show,
Then off they went, all in a row!

So here I sit with dampened dreams,
Nothing is quite as it seems.
Maybe tomorrow I'll try again,
Or just stay home and watch my hen.

A Day Spun in Gold

Woke up to a sunbeam's kiss,
Fried an egg, oh what a bliss!
Spilled my juice, it made a rainbow,
My breakfast turned into a show!

Off to work, dressed like a king,
Stumbled on my shoelace string.
Tripped right into a paper stack,
My papers flew—now there's no track!

Meetings piled like dirty dishes,
With dreams of fish and little wishes.
A coffee spill, oh what a scene,
It's just another day, you know what I mean?

Home at last, the couch awaits,
Time to unstick from my fates.
Tomorrow brings its silver thread,
But tonight, it's just me and the bread!

Veils of Snow and Memories

Snowflakes dance like little sprites,
In winter's chill, oh what delight!
I tried to build a snowman tight,
But ended up in a snowy fight!

Lost my scarf in a frosty breeze,
Chased it down with snow-filled knees.
Made a friend from frozen flake,
We giggled loud, then tried to bake!

In the kitchen, oh what a mess,
Flour flew like winter's dress.
The cookies burned, what a delight,
Guess we'll feast on snow tonight!

As night falls, the stars peep through,
I sip my cocoa, feeling blue.
But laughter echoes in the air,
Snowy memories, beyond compare!

Morning Starlight and Wishes

Woke up early, the stars still shone,
Stumbled out of bed, I'm not alone.
A cat on my head, what a sight,
What can I wish for? Maybe a bite!

The coffee brewed, but it's clouded,
I poured it out, just feeling clouded.
Crabs in my socks? You can't be true!
Oh wait, that's just my morning zoo!

Chasing dreams that fly away,
Fell down hard, what can I say?
A wish on a star, I'll give it a go,
"Please bring me breakfast, or maybe a show!"

The day begins with a flip and spin,
Life's a circus, let the fun begin!
With morning starlight shining bright,
Let's make more wishes with all our might!

Caroling Clouds Above

The clouds sing carols in the sky,
Dancing with joy, oh my, oh my!
They've got rhythm, they've got cheer,
Spreading giggles far and near.

They wear bright hats made of fluff,
Puffing out tunes that are quite tough.
A cloud in green, a cloud in red,
Hilarious songs from their fluffy heads.

Raindrops join in on saxophones,
While thunder claps and moans in tones.
Who knew clouds had such great flair?
Weather forecasts? They don't care!

With snowflakes dancing cheek to cheek,
They throw snowballs and play hide and seek.
In this sky, there's never a frown,
Just caroling clouds, wearing their crown.

Mistletoe Murmurs at Sunrise

Under mistletoe, bears shuffle and sway,
Whispers of secrets in a funny way.
They kiss like it's just a bear thing,
While squirrels giggle, and birds take wing.

At sunrise, laughter fills the air,
With cheeky bets and wintry dare.
The sunlight spills like syrup on toast,
Bears proclaiming, "We're the most!"

Frogs croak tunes in a slick ballet,
While rabbits hop in a silly display.
"Just two more nips," a bear would decree,
And the branches shake with pure glee!

With every murmur, feasts come alive,
From berry pies to honey, they thrive.
Nature's jesters at sunrise gleam,
In this mistletoe madness, we dream.

Fireside Flickers and Fond Memories

Fireside flickers dance with the light,
Whispers of stories, all cozy and bright.
Grandpa tells tales of his socks so old,
How they stood guard, brave and bold!

With marshmallows roasting, a gooey delight,
Last year's s'mores ignite a big fight.
Who took the last one? Oh, what a scene!
The flames jump higher, the chaos is keen.

The cat in the corner, plotting a scheme,
To snatch the last treat, that sneaky little dream.
Dogs yawn and stretch, dreaming of snack,
While grandkids giggle, never looking back.

With every ember, laughter gets loud,
We're lost in our memories, who's ever allowed!
Fireside flickers, warm tales entwine,
Each crackle a memory, truly divine.

Gentle Waking of the Season

The season wakes with a yawn and a stretch,
Chirping in chorus, with joy they fetch.
Squirrels wear hats made of fallen leaves,
Tickling the air as everyone believes.

Gentle breezes whisper secrets so sweet,
Turning the leaves into friends we'd meet.
"Let's play tag!" a little fox cries,
As the sun peeks in with sleepy eyes.

Frogs jump high, they leap with delight,
While bunnies hop with sheer delight.
Dancing with daisies, it's quite the sight,
Each day a new game beneath morning light.

As winter tiptoes, with giggles galore,
The gentler season brings joy to the floor.
So here we are, with hearts all aglow,
In the gentle waking, let laughter flow.

Lullabies of a Winter's Day

Snowflakes dance like fairy sprites,
Cold air steals away our bites.
Under blankets, warm we lay,
Dreaming of that sunny day.

Sipping cocoa, marshmallows float,
While outside, snowmen wear a coat.
Frosty noses, rosy cheeks,
Winter's charm, oh how it speaks!

Beneath the stars, our laughter rings,
Snowball fights are the best of things.
The dog has slipped and gone for a roll,
Winter's joy, it warms the soul.

So sing a song to winter's chill,
With joy and silliness, we refill.
Lullabies of snow and fun,
As winter's day is nearly done.

Sights and Smells of Sweet Delights

In the bakery, the cookies call,
Chocolate chip, they'll make you fall.
Frosted cakes and pies so bright,
Confections that will ignite delight.

Cotton candy, spun so sweet,
Marshmallow fluff, such a treat.
Caramel drips and fruit galore,
Sights and smells, we crave for more.

Cookies baking, oh what a scent,
Whipped cream clouds, we're heaven-bent.
With every bite, our smiles grow wide,
In this sweet world, we take a ride.

So raise your forks, let's dig right in,
Each dessert just makes us grin.
With sights and smells that tease our fate,
In sweet delights, we celebrate!

The First Footfall on Soft Snow

The first footfall on soft snow,
Crunching sounds as cold winds blow.
Wearing boots, a careful tread,
Following the path ahead.

Snowflakes land upon my nose,
Dancing down like tiny prose.
With every step, a silly slip,
Oh dear, down I go with a flip!

Building forts with snowy walls,
We're the kings of winter halls.
Snowmen wear our funny hats,
Laughing loud, we're all like cats.

So take a leap, embrace the chill,
Chase the laughter, embrace the thrill.
With every footfall, joy connects,
The first of snow brings sweet effects!

A Blanket of Stars and Wishes

Under the sky, a blanket laid,
Stars above, like wishes made.
Each twinkle tells a silly tale,
Of dancing fish and clever snails.

Moonbeams casting shadows bright,
Dreams take flight in the night.
With wishes whispered out so loud,
We float on dreams, a fluffy cloud.

Holding hands, we count them fast,
Stars, like candies, too good to last.
With laughter shared, our hearts entwine,
In this vast cosmic design.

So close your eyes and make a plea,
For ice cream treats and lots of glee.
A blanket of stars, our night's delight,
Where wishes flourish in soft moonlight.

Kindles in the Quietude

In the quietude of night,
A light shines oh so bright,
Kindles flicker in their place,
Chasing shadows all my grace.

Whispers of the books we read,
Kittens curling, hearts to feed,
Ghosts of stories laugh and play,
Turning pages, here we stay.

Chocolate crumbs on every shelf,
Reading tales of someone else,
Snoring loud, my cat's a star,
Dreams of space, oh how bizarre!

So here we sit, a comfy crew,
Sipping cocoa, feeling new,
Kindles glow and laughter flies,
In this world, we are the wise.

Hearthside Stories in Winter's Embrace

Winter whispers, snowflakes fall,
Gather 'round, we'll tell them all,
Stories from the hearth so bright,
Muffin crumbs and pure delight.

Uncles snore, aunties giggle,
Stockings hung, we dance and wiggle,
Grandpa's tales of yore unfold,
Santa's trip, a sight to hold.

Freckles, pets, and sledding woes,
Hot cocoa, silly winter clothes,
Laughter echoes, children cheer,
Winter's magic, ever near.

So let's toast to stories grand,
By the fire, hand in hand,
Winter's chill can't dampen fun,
Hearthside tales for everyone!

A Symphony of Sweets and Smiles

In the kitchen, oh what bliss,
Cookies baked, you sure can't miss,
Sprinkles dance and chocolate sings,
Joyful hearts, we're all like kings.

Brownies gooey, icing bright,
Sweets are calling, oh what a sight,
Lollipops and cakes galore,
Every flavor, we explore.

Laughter echoes from the bowls,
Tummy grumbling, hungry souls,
Meringues soaring in the air,
Sugar rush, we do not care!

So grab a treat, share a grin,
In this symphony, we win,
Sweets and smiles, a perfect mix,
Join the fun, it's time for kicks!

A Melody of Giving Hearts

When the stars begin to shine,
Kindness flows, it feels divine,
Giving hearts with open hands,
Spreading love across the lands.

Random acts, a little cheer,
Taking time to lend an ear,
Sharing snacks or heartfelt notes,
Simple gifts, like little boats.

Laughter sparks and joy takes flight,
In our hearts, it feels so right,
Every smile, a melody,
Together strong, just you and me.

So let's dance in this delight,
Turn our hearts into the light,
With giving spirits leading the way,
We'll share this love, come what may!

Evergreen Echoes at Daybreak

In the woods where squirrels play,
They dance and prance, oh what a display,
With acorns flying left and right,
They're plotting snacks for their big night.

The sun wakes up with a yawn,
A sleepy glow, a golden dawn,
Birds start chirping, they take their flight,
While rabbits hop in sheer delight.

Trees stretch up in morning cheer,
With branches waving, 'Come near, come near!'
The mossy ground gives a little shake,
As if to say, 'Awake! For goodness' sake!'

So here we are in nature's show,
With giggles shared as breezes blow,
Let's laugh aloud, shake off the drowsy,
In evergreen echoes, life's just so squeezy!

Red Ribbons and Golden Wishes

In a shop where dreams come true,
Red ribbons tied, just for you,
Golden wishes upon a star,
Or maybe just a cookie jar.

Sell me luck, I'll take a chance,
And maybe get up to some dance,
A twist of fate, a flurry of glee,
With ribbons wrapped around my tea.

A hiccup here, a giggle there,
Chocolate sprinkles in my hair,
I wish for quirks, I wish for fun,
Under the warmth of the golden sun.

With every bow, my heart will smile,
Let's stay silly for a while,
In this tale, we're free to play,
With red ribbons leading the way!

Frost-Kissed Kisses

Oh winter's breath, a crisp delight,
When snowflakes fall, a snowy sight,
With frosty kisses on my nose,
I laugh and yell, 'Look at those toes!'

The chilly air makes cheeks turn pink,
Hot cocoa ready, let's not blink,
We'll build a snowman, tall and round,
And decorate him with an old crown.

A slippery slide down the hill,
With giggles loud and hearts to fill,
A snowball fight erupts, oh joy!
A frosty bash for every girl and boy.

So let it snow, let's dance and sing,
With frost-kissed love, oh what a fling,
Winter's magic never misses,
Our hearts aglow with frosty kisses!

A Tapestry of Tidings

In a world where quirk meets cheer,
A tapestry of laughter's near,
With threads of joy and a splash of fun,
Together we weave, oh what a run!

From tangled threads, a story spun,
Of curious cats and a golden bun,
With every loop, a giggle grows,
As the fabric of friendship softly glows.

So let's create a patchwork bright,
With silly patterns, a pure delight,
In every stitch, a tale to share,
Woven together, beyond compare.

In this tapestry, we find our place,
With laughter stitched in every space,
A quilt of joy, forever binding,
In a world where love is blinding!

Heartstrings of Yuletide Cheer

When Santa's sleigh is stuck in snow,
He blames the reindeer, 'What a show!'
The cookies left are all but gone,
But he won't share his midnight brawn.

The lights we hung are tangled tight,
We thought we'd do this, oh, what a sight!
Dad's on the roof, in holiday gear,
With one false step, he's got no cheer!

Our tree leans left, it's quite bizarre,
Nana swears it'll find a star.
The ornaments are all in place,
Except for one, it's lost its face.

In Christmas songs, the best part's here,
When Frosty starts to shed a tear.
But worry not, for hot cocoa flows,
And we'll fake cheer until it snows!

Reflections in a Cup of Cocoa

In a mug so large, I float a sweet,
With marshmallows that dance, oh what a treat!
I sip and slurp, it's pure delight,
While visions of fudge give me a fright.

My cocoa's thick, like a winter night,
I swear it gives me super sight!
I see the cat, plotting a strike,
For my cookies! Oh, hiss and bike!

The whipped cream mountains rise so tall,
I fear I might just lose it all.
As sprinkles rain down from the pouch,
I'm now the happiest cocoa grouch!

Each slurp a dream, it's cocoa flair,
But I must save some for the fair.
So here's my call, before it's gone,
To all my friends, ye merry throng!

Moments Beneath the Evergreen

Beneath the tree, the gifts grow high,
I peek and poke, oh me, oh my!
A present wrapped with sparkly tape,
Is it a game, or is it a cape?

Grandpa snores with a holiday hat,
While grandma's found a comfy mat.
The dog's in the box, a gift gone rogue,
He wiggles and wags, an innocent brogue.

We sing songs that are out of tune,
While Auntie twirls like a sugar moon.
The punch explodes, it's a crimson scene,
We laugh and spill, the merriest sheen.

Underneath the boughs, we snicker and cheer,
For moments like these, we're glad you are here.
With laughter and joy, we gather and sing,
For Christmas is more than just bling!

Glimmers of Hope on Frosty Eves

On frosty eves, the stars are bright,
We roast marshmallows, such a sight!
With s'mores that stick to the roof of my mouth,
I giggle and grin, oh, what a spout!

A snowman wobbles, he waves with glee,
Till a squirrel steals his nose, oh, wee!
"Not my carrot!" the children cry,
As they chase the critter and sigh oh my!

The hot tea spills, a winter tale,
Of snowflakes that dance, we set our sail.
We gather 'round, with hearts aglow,
And whisper dreams beneath the snow.

As peppermint swirls fill the night,
We smile wide, feeling just right.
For glimmers of hope keep us warm,
In frosty eves, we break the norm!

Snowflakes and Silent Lullabies

Snowflakes dance in the chilly breeze,
Whispering secrets like old trees.
They land on my nose, I giggle with glee,
Oh, winter's magic, just let it be!

Sipping some cocoa, it's spiced just right,
The marshmallows float, oh what a sight!
Outside, kids tumble, snowballs in flight,
Silent lulled dreams on this frosty night.

Cats wear sweaters, looking quite dapper,
While dogs wear scarves, oh what a caper!
A snowman winks, a real head turner,
With carrots for noses, they're all a winner!

As snowflakes twirl, the world feels so grand,
Join the laughing brigade, lend a hand!
In winter's embrace, together we stand,
Snowflakes and lullabies, perfectly planned.

A Serenade for December

December comes, the chill in the air,
Sipping on cider, it's time for a dare!
Sing to the snowmen, let laughter be shared,
In frosty attire, you know that we've dared!

With mittens and scarves, we stumble and glide,
Slipping on ice, oh, take it in stride!
The carolers croon with melted delight,
While snowflakes giggle and twinkle at night.

Nutmeg and cinnamon in every pot,
Baking those cookies, the sugar's not shot!
"Just one more," we say, but we're all tied in knots,
The scales will be glaring, oh what a thought!

But laughter is gold, it's the warmth we adore,
So raise up a glass, let's feast and explore!
In December's embrace, let joy be our core,
A serenade of laughter, forevermore!

Morning's First Light on Frosted Fields

Morning breaks soft on frosted fields,
The grass wears ice like a magical shield.
Chickens are clucking, they're feeling quite bold,
"Where's my breakfast?" they scratch, the sight's quite gold!

Sunbeams flicker, then playfully dance,
Casting long shadows, let's give it a chance.
A pancake flip shows off my fine stance,
But syrup goes splat! Oh, culinary romance!

The coffee is brewing; it smells like a dream,
I trip on a toy, hear the house cat's scream.
Barefoot on tiles, oh what a theme,
If laughter's the goal, I'm a morning meme!

Yet still, here's the bliss in this frosty morn,
Mirth fills the air like a blanket well-worn.
With warmth in my heart, and giggles reborn,
Morning's first light is a tale to adorn.

Cinnamon Dreams in the Air

Cinnamon dreams waft through the room,
With gingerbread houses, they break the gloom.
Sugar and spice, oh give me a break,
I'm diving in frosting, for goodness' sake!

Shoveling cookies, oh what a feat,
Sprinkles fly high in a sugar sweet treat.
With flour on noses, we laugh and we cheer,
In this holiday madness, there's nothing to fear!

Merry tunes play while we dance on the floor,
Twisting around, oh, please give me more!
The stockings are stuffed, and the tree is aglow,
Cinnamon dreams swirl in a delightful flow!

So here's to the laughter, the joy, and the fun,
As we bake a batch 'til the daylight is done.
In kitchens of laughter, our hearts will run,
Cinnamon dreams in the air, we have won!

Hearthside Hues of Happiness

The fire crackles, pops, and snaps,
Marshmallows dance, and so do my laps.
Cats knock over the lanterns with glee,
While I'm tripping over my own cup of tea.

Laughter bounces off the walls so bright,
Silly jokes fired until late at night.
Mom's secret cookies, I'll take a big bite,
Gaining weight's worth it; they taste just right!

The pillows are flying, it's soft as can be,
We're all just a bunch of big kids, you see.
With slippers that squeak and blankets to share,
This hearthside is heaven, we've not a care!

So grab your hot cocoa, and join the fun,
The warmth in this room is second to none.
Sitting together is truly the best,
In hues of pure happiness, we're blessed!

Sunlight Dancing on Ice

The sun peeks out, a mischievous guide,
As ice skaters slip and take awkward dives.
With the grace of a penguin, I join in the fun,
And flail like a fish as bright as the sun!

Snowflakes twirl down, just like a dance,
While I stumble and fall, never a chance.
But that's how it goes on a bright wintry day,
When laughter erupts as we tumble and sway.

Hot chocolate in hand, I cherish the view,
Teetering on skates like I'm new to the zoo.
But friends all around me, we wobble and glide,
With sunlight dancing, we're filled with pride!

In this frosty world, we chase away fears,
With giggles and smiles, we toast with our cheers.
Sunlight on ice, a day to recall,
Though my balance is shaky, I'm having a ball!

Memories Frozen in Time

With every snapshot, we pause and we grin,
Caught in a moment, let the fun begin!
You'll see us goofing, with silly hairdos,
Pouting like llamas in our bright colored shoes.

Cringing at hairstyles from years long ago,
Or my uncle's dance moves – oh, what a show!
Yet each frozen memory brings warmth to my heart,
From birthday cake mess to the family art.

Grandma's wild stories that never grow old,
In photos and laughter, they shimmer like gold.
We laugh 'til we cry, then we cry a bit more,
With a love that we treasure, that's all we adore!

So we gather again, with a camera in hand,
To capture these moments, together we stand.
Life's quirks and its wonders, all perfectly chime,
With memories frozen, we savor each time!

Unwrapping the Day's Delights

As morning breaks with a muffin in hand,
I unravel the goodness of breakfast so grand.
Eggs dance with bacon, a sizzle so fine,
It's a tasty parade, and I'm first in the line!

With laughter and giggles, my coffee's a friend,
I sip through the chaos that mornings may send.
Sneaky sock gnomes hide things all around,
But today, oh delight! They've left joy to be found.

The afternoon brings snacks with a crunch,
Ice cream conspired to be part of the bunch.
We unwrap the flavors in a glorious way,
Candy wrappers flying as we laugh and we play.

As sunsets arrive with a wink and a twirl,
I unwrap the memories; they make my heart whirl.
Each moment a treasure, each laugh a delight,
Unwrapping the day's joys, I'm ready for night!

Whispers of Peace and Togetherness

In a world of chaos, we take a breath,
Sharing our snacks, avoiding the lettuce.
Laughter echoes in this cozy space,
With peace in our hearts, and crumbs on our face.

United we stand with pizza in hand,
Bickering over toppings, it's perfectly planned.
Harmony found in each playful fight,
Who knew togetherness could be such a bite!

As we break bread, the world feels light,
Even this cat thinks we're doing it right.
We toast with our glasses, raised high with glee,
A group hug for all, even Fido agrees!

So come join this feast, let laughter ensue,
Whispers of joy, our secret brew.
In the warmth of together, love overshadows,
Chasing away worries, like warm fluffy shadows.

Morning Chimes of Festive Voices

Dawn breaks gently, coffee's our friend,
The early birds sing, let the fun never end.
With pancakes piled high and syrup galore,
We dance in our jammies, who could ask for more?

Chimes in the kitchen, pots start to clang,
A egg-splosion occurs; oh, what a fang!
We wave at the neighbors, in pajamas so bright,
Morning chimes of laughter start a silly fight!

The toast flies high like a toast-master's dream,
Cream cheese on the counter, it's all quite a scene.
With voices so merry, our hearts feel alive,
In the laughter of morning, our spirits thrive!

So let's cheer to breakfast, a feast we'll create,
With eggs, and jam, and laughter on plate.
Together we rise like the sun in the sky,
Morning chimes of joy; we can never be shy!

A Palette of Possibilities

With crayons and giggles, we color the day,
Mixing all shades in a wacky array.
Draw a cat with a hat and a bike on a tree,
Who says art needs rules? Not you and not me!

Splashes of laughter on canvas appear,
Paintbrushes twirl like a wild cavalier.
We dab and we smudge in a flurry of glee,
A masterpiece birthed—it's a sight to see!

Chaos and colors create a delight,
A rainbow erupts in the soft morning light.
In this palette of joy, creativity flows,
With silly designs that nobody knows!

So gather your colors and unleash the fun,
In a vibrant adventure, time stands still—none!
Each stroke tells a story, each giggle's a spree,
A palette of possibilities; come paint life with me!

Glimmers of Gratefulness at Dawn

As dawn tiptoes in, we take a deep sigh,
Thankful for coffee and donuts nearby.
The sun peeks over, a cheeky good morn,
Gratefulness glimmers with each day reborn.

With slippers so cozy, we shuffle around,
Giving thanks to the toaster that doesn't make a sound.
Blessings stacked high like a plate full of bread,
For every odd moment, a giggle instead!

Nature's a beauty, the flowers attest,
Even the squirrels say we're truly the best.
We raise our mugs high, a toast to the bliss,
Gratefulness dances in every warm kiss!

So cherish the dawn with its shimmering glow,
In the hustle of life, let your thankfulness grow.
For each little moment, let gratitude sing,
Glimmers of joy as a new day takes wing!

Silent Carols in the Air

In a world where silence weaves,
The carolers lost their singing leaves.
Whispers float, a tune so rare,
But not a note could fill the air.

Snowmen gather, looking prim,
One forgot his hat, oh what a whim!
Chimneys puff their smoke so clear,
But no one knows who's singing here.

Mistletoe Memories at Sunrise

Under mistletoe, a bold embrace,
But then I trip and fall on my face.
The kiss was sweet, but I confess,
Now I'm blushing in my Sunday dress.

Sunrise brings a brand new day,
With coffee spills, hip hip hooray!
Forgot my keys and lost my hat,
Now I'm late for work, how about that?

A Hearth's Warm Embrace

The hearth crackles, a warm delight,
But I burnt my toast and it took flight.
Marshmallows roasting, oh what fun,
Till one leaped out, just my luck, done!

Socks are stashed, all cozy and neat,
But one's missing, and it's a feat!
I search high and low, what a chase,
Turns out it's hiding in my vase!

Snowflakes Dance on Windowpanes

Snowflakes twirl, a frosty ballet,
But my nose is red, what can I say?
They gather round with graceful flair,
I catch one, now it's in my hair!

A snowball fight, a victory scream,
But I hit my friend, oh what a dream!
Now we're laughing, covered in white,
Who knew winter could feel so right?

The Glow of Hopeful Hearts

In the glow of hopeful hearts,
We stumble on our way,
Like fireflies in the dark,
Chasing dreams that stray.

Our future's bright and shiny,
Yet socks keep disappearing,
We smile through all the chaos,
While our pants keep reappearing.

With every laugh and silly joke,
We light the darkest night,
For hope is just a wink away,
Bringing giggles with delight.

So raise a glass of fizzy cheer,
To friendships we hold dear,
With goofy grins and dances grand,
We conquer every fear.

Sleigh Bells Sounding Softly

Sleigh bells ringing oh so sweet,
In the snow we stomp our feet,
With cocoa in our hands we cheer,
As snowflakes dance from far and near.

Rudolph's nose, it shines so bright,
Guiding us through the frosty night,
Yet somehow we've lost the way,
And now we're stuck in a snowdrift's sway.

With laughter bouncing off the trees,
We build a snowman with such ease,
His button eyes in a cheeky stare,
With a carrot nose and messy hair.

So let's embrace the winter's fun,
With snowball fights till we're all done,
For sleigh bells sound, and we will play,
Until the break of Christmas Day.

Starlit Pathways to Warmth

Starlit pathways guide our feet,
While we argue which treat's a cheat,
With cookies warm, our hands we warm,
As we gather round for stories to form.

The stars above don't seem to mind,
Our goofy antics, well-defined,
For every laugh lights up the night,
Making our hearts feel just right.

Under twinkling lights, we sway,
With goofy grins, we lose our way,
Yet in this joyful, merry haze,
We find our warmth in holiday ways.

So come and join this silly dance,
Together we'll take a daring chance,
For starlit pathways lead us home,
Where laughter and love will always roam.

Joy Wrapped in Handmade Love

Joy wrapped in handmade love,
A gift that fits just like a glove,
With glitter, glue, and lots of flair,
We craft our dreams with utmost care.

Our presents may not always shine,
But hey, they're made with love divine,
A mug that's chipped, a scarf that's bright,
All wrapped up in sheer delight.

Each ribbon tied with silly knots,
Reminds us of all the happy spots,
Cause love's the best gift that we share,
While giggles float around in the air.

So let's embrace this crafty glow,
With playful hearts, we steal the show,
For joy wrapped in handmade love,
Is the greatest gift sent from above.

Sweet Serenades Beneath the Boughs

A squirrel strummed his tiny lute,
While birds joined in, oh what a hoot!
They sang of nuts and sunny skies,
With melodies that made us rise.

The trees danced along with glee,
As rabbits twirled in jubilee.
Each note a laugh, each chord a cheer,
Nature's concert, loud and clear!

A deer with shades, so cool and slick,
Joined the band with a little trick.
He tapped his hooves, the crowd went wild,
As squirrels laughed, the forest smiled.

So if you hear a tune today,
Just follow the sound, don't delay.
Sweet serenades beneath those boughs,
Are nature's gift; let's take a bow!

Warm Wishes in the Cold

Frosty mornings make us shiver,
While hot cocoa makes us quiver.
With marshmallows floating high,
We laugh and sip, oh me, oh my!

The snowflakes dance like tiny sprites,
While penguins wobble in their sights.
In mittens fluffier than a cloud,
We giggle and stomp, feeling proud.

Let's build a snowman, fat and round,
With a carrot nose that's renowned!
As we throw snowballs, aiming wide,
Laughter echoes—our hearts' joyride!

So warm wishes as the snowflakes fall,
Let's spread the cheer, let's have a ball!
For in the cold, we're snug and bold,
Together we shine, like treasure untold!

Starry Nights, Merry Mornings

The stars twinkle like eyes aglow,
As night whispers secrets we all know.
Dreams ride on the beams of light,
In the stillness of the night so bright.

Morning arrives with a cheerful grin,
As coffee brews, our day begins.
The toast pops up, a little dance,
Who knew breakfast could be a chance?

Cats chase sunbeams, dogs bark away,
The joys of morning, the start of play.
We trip on shoes and spill our juice,
But laugh it off, who's got a recluse?

Starry nights and merry days,
Let's embrace life in a funny craze!
For every twinkle up above,
Holds a story of laughter and love!

Twinkling Lights and Gentle Dreams

Twinkling lights on the tree aglow,
Reflect the joy in the hearts below.
With tinsel here and garland there,
A festive spirit fills the air.

Gentle dreams dance in our heads,
Of cookies, laughter, and cozy beds.
As stockings hang, we make a list,
Of all the hugs we can't resist.

The cat's on the tree, oh what a sight!
Trying to reach those ornaments bright.
While children giggle, as they peek,
At Santa's sleigh hiding by the creek.

So let's light up the night with cheer,
And spread good wishes far and near.
For twinkling lights and dreams so sweet,
Make every moment feel complete!

A Canvas of Colors: Red and Green

Red is for the apples that fall from the trees,
Green is for the broccoli that gives us the squeeze.
A salad's a party, with colors galore,
But dressing it up? That's a challenge for sure.

Christmas lights twinkle, all tangled in cheer,
While Rudolph's chasing carrots, oh dear, oh dear!
Red and green together, it's quite the display,
Who knew veggies could make us laugh in this way?

A tomato's a fruit, but with salad it fights,
While I just try to keep my veggies in tights.
Red peppers are spicy, green ones are mild,
Both hop on my plate, and I'm back to the wild.

So here's to the colors, a vibrant delight,
In bowls and in smiles, they make everything bright.
With red and with green, let's make a parade,
And dance through the kitchen, our fears all outweigh!

Joyous Tidings in Every Corner

Joyful tidings ring, though my cat's on my head,
She thinks I'm a cushion, but I'm not, I have said!
Happiness spreads like the jam on my toast,
But is more like the coffee that I like the most.

Mice dance in the pantry, rats twirl in the fridge,
Where's my little snack? It vanished like magic!
I shout out to the neighbors with cheer and delight,
But they're all just asleep, not a soul in sight.

The dog digs a hole, his smile full of glee,
While I'm trying to teach him, "Just let it be free!"
Joyous moments weave, like spaghetti on plates,
Why can't I find joy in these potato debates?

So here's to the laughter, the silliness reigns,
In every corner of life, through joy and through pains.
The cat on my head, the dog in the yard,
These joyful tidings? I'll keep them, they're starred!

Golden Glimmers of Grateful Hearts

Golden glimmers shine from every little smile,
Like pancakes at dawn, oh, they're worth the while!
Grateful hearts are full of syrupy delight,
But first, we must find the butter, that's right!

With friends gathered round, and laughter in air,
Each moment we cherish, with love we declare.
Gratitude's like a pie, it's best when it's shared,
But if you take a big slice, we might be impaired.

A hug's like a donut, with sprinkles on top,
It cheers up our days, and we'll never stop.
Golden moments shimmer, like fireflies at night,
They brighten our souls, oh, what a sweet sight!

So here's to the golden, the funny, the sweet,
The joy of our friendships, they can't be beat.
In grateful hearts whisper, let's cheer with a laugh,
For the syrupy sweetness is our biggest half!

The Embrace of Winter's Breath

Winter's breath is chilly, oh what a surprise,
With snowflakes that tickle and frostbite that pries.
Hot cocoa is waiting, a friend in a mug,
To warm up my fingers, like hugging a bug.

Snowmen are flopping, their smiles are all sad,
They're losing their noses, it's making me mad!
But laughs fill the air with each slip on the ice,
A dance move gone wrong? Oh, how very nice!

The nights are so long, like my cousin's tall tales,
With stories of snowstorms and fantastical gales.
Yet, blankets of white bring some cheer and some fun,
As we watch the flakes swirl down, one by one!

So let's bundle up tight and embrace winter's chill,
With laughter, hot chocolate, and maybe a thrill.
For life's greatest joys can be found in the cold,
In the warmth of our hearts, where each story is told!

Frost-kissed Dreams and Golden Rays

A snowman danced with his carrot nose,
While penguins wear shorts, striking silly poses.
Sunbeams on ice, what a goofy sight,
Nature's own joke, oh what pure delight!

Sledding down hills, we scream and we fly,
With hot cocoa spills, oh me, oh my!
A snowball fight starts, it's chaos and cheer,
With laughter and shrieks that we hold oh so dear.

Frosty the snowman decided to sing,
But ended up sounding like a rusty old spring.
Golden rays captured in a jolly embrace,
As we trip on our sleds in this hilarious race!

So here's to the winter, warm hearts we'll find,
In frosty dreams leaving worries behind.
With golden rays shining, all stress will erase,
Join us for laughs in this crazy cold space!

Serenity in the Embrace of Winter

Snowflakes are falling, they start their ballet,
Each twirl doing pirouettes in the fray.
Children in snow suits look like marshmallows,
Tumbling around, their giggles like bellows!

Icicles hang like nature's chandeliers,
But watch out below, as they shed their spears!
Winter's embrace feels like a warm hug,
Until you slip on ice, then it's a total shrug.

The fireplace crackles with a comforting roar,
But the cat's on the mantel, plotting to score.
Chasing that warmth, while dogs run amok,
Winter's calm moments are made of pure luck!

With hot soup that's steamier than a dance floor,
And socks on our hands, who needs to explore?
Cozied up tight, we'll navigate this fate,
With laughter and joy, our hearts will elate!

Whispers of Winter's Dawn

Morning unfolds with a blanket of frost,
Hot chocolate bubbles, oh what a cost!
A squirrel in pajamas dashes for snacks,
While snow plows rumble, leaving huge tracks.

The sun peeks out, what a silly tease,
Melting down snowflakes to puddles with ease.
Oh, the chubby snowman's lost half of his head,
He's just another victim of weather, it's said.

With winter birds chirping a sweet serenade,
They're gossiping 'bout pancakes, how they're homemade.
Frosty the snowman, he's losing his charm,
With each passing hour, it's a low-key alarm!

But we bring out the sleds and the laughter will fly,
As we race down the hill, underneath the wide sky.
Whispers of winter, our joy will persist,
As we frolic in snow; how could we resist?

Gifts Wrapped in Glimmers

Presents so shiny, they twinkle and glow,
But watch who unwrapped them; you better not show!
The dog found the cookies and made quite a mess,
With crumbs on his face, it's hard to confess.

Lights on the tree blink like a disco ball,
As we dance through the room, tripping over it all.
A cat in the tinsel, quite proud of his throne,
As gifts start exploding from bad wrapping alone.

Wreaths on the doors yelling 'Happy and Bright!'
While kids run around wrapped in paper, what a sight!
Laughter is echoing through every hall,
As we wrestle with ribbons until someone falls.

So here's to the chaos, the giggles, the cheer,
With gifts wrapped in glimmers, we hold dear!
As winter unfolds with its magical spin,
We celebrate life, let the fun times begin!

Milton Keynes UK
Ingram Content Group UK Ltd.
UKHW022122091224
452185UK00010B/466

9 789916 909393

Original title:
The Strength to Let Go

Copyright © 2024 Swan Charm
All rights reserved.

Author: Liisi Lendorav
ISBN HARDBACK: 978-9916-89-709-6
ISBN PAPERBACK: 978-9916-89-710-2
ISBN EBOOK: 978-9916-89-711-9

Surrender to the Celestial Plan

In shadows deep, I hear the call,
A whisper soft, to one and all.
With humble heart, I bend my knee,
Embracing grace, I long to be.

The stars above, they light my way,
In every night, in every day.
Divine design, so vast and grand,
I trust my soul to heaven's hand.

Through trials faced, I find my peace,
In letting go, my doubts release.
For in the storm, there's calm within,
A sacred space where love begins.

With open arms, I welcome fate,
Each step I take, I consecrate.
The journey strange, yet still I tread,
With faith as my eternal thread.

In silence deep, I hear the grace,
A gentle guide, in time and space.
Surrender sweet, to what shall be,
In harmony, my spirit free.

When the Soul Takes Flight

In the silence, angels sing,
Heavenly whispers take to wing.
Lost in prayer, the spirit soars,
Beyond the realms, where joy restores.

Hearts aflame, the light descends,
Bringing peace as sorrow ends.
In the stillness, grace abides,
As the soul in love resides.

Cherished Moments Left Behind

In the echoes of sunset's glow,
Memories linger, soft and low.
Faithful shadows dance in light,
Carrying whispers of the night.

Each moment, like a fleeting prayer,
Holds the love we used to share.
Time unravels yet remains,
In the heart, where hope sustains.

Epiphany in the Absence

In the void where silence dwells,
Wisdom flows and truth compels.
Seeking solace in the dark,
Finding strength in each new spark.

With every loss, a lesson gained,
In our hearts, the love remains.
Through the tears, we learn to see,
The light reflected endlessly.

Wings Clipped Yet Soaring Free

Bound by fate, yet spirits rise,
In silent prayer, we seek the skies.
Limitations cannot confine,
The sacred dreams, our souls align.

In the struggle, grace appears,
Carving strength from deepest fears.
Though the body bears the weight,
The heart transcends, embracing fate.

Wings of Release

In the quiet dusk, we seek the light,
The whispers of grace, guiding our flight.
With every breath, we shed our fears,
As faith unfurls, like wings of tears.

The heavens call, a gentle sound,
In surrender's fold, our hearts are bound.
We rise above, where shadows cease,
In the embrace of divine peace.

The Altar of Farewell

At the altar's edge, we lay our trust,
In moments cherished, in sacred dust.
With tearful prayers, we bid adieu,
To all that's known, and what is true.

In the quiet space, where echoes blend,
We hold the memories that never end.
As hearts unite, though paths may part,
Love's gentle song plays on in the heart.

Echoes of Surrender

In the silence deep, a voice is heard,
A promise woven in every word.
As we let go, the weight we bear,
In trusting arms, we've found our prayer.

Through trials faced, we find our way,
In the darkest night, there comes the day.
With every step, in faith we sway,
In echoes of surrender, we choose to stay.

Faithful Departures

With every parting, a journey starts,
In the quiet whispers of tender hearts.
As wings are lifted, we learn to trust,
In the hands of fate, we find our crust.

In loving bonds that never fray,
We carry love beyond the day.
Through faithful departures, hope is sown,
In the depths of love, we're never alone.

Celestial Streams of Urgency

In the glow of dusk, we gather,
Voices rise like whispers sent,
Heaven's call, a sacred flutter,
Guiding souls where hope is meant.

Stars align, a cosmic dance,
Each heartbeat, a rhythm drawn,
Faith ignites, a vibrant trance,
Light emerging at each dawn.

Winds of grace, they swirl and weave,
Threads of mercy, softly spun,
In this space, we dare believe,
The work of love has just begun.

Mountains high, valleys deep,
Every challenge meets the sky,
In our hearts, the promise keeps,
Tears of joy when we reply.

Flowing waters, pure and clear,
Bathe the spirit, soothe the soul,
In this realm, we have no fear,
Celestial streams will make us whole.

Gentle Release in Hidden Prayers

In the silence, hearts unfold,
Whispers rise on wings of grace,
Hope and solace, gently told,
In tucked corners, we embrace.

Words unspoken, thoughts released,
Fingers clasped in sacred hush,
In this stillness, doubts are ceased,
Divine presence in each rush.

Beneath the veil, we often find,
Hidden prayers, a quiet sigh,
Tender moments, softly bind,
In the shadows, love draws nigh.

A flicker glows, a candle's light,
Guiding us through darkest times,
In the gloom, we claim our right,
To find peace in whispered rhymes.

Eyes closed tight, we breathe in deep,
Each exhale a letting go,
In this journey, faith will reap,
Gentle release, a sacred flow.

The Path of Unraveled Threads

Step by step, the journey's told,
Threads of fate, woven tight,
In the tapestry, bright and bold,
Each choice a spark igniting light.

Mountains rise, rivers bend,
Every twist a lesson learned,
In the end, hearts will mend,
From those moments, wisdom earned.

Through the struggle, strength will show,
In every fray, a chance to grow,
With each unravel, we let go,
Path revealed, as spirits flow.

Voices echo from the past,
Stories rich, they guide us still,
In their shadows, shadows cast,
Feet will follow, guided will.

In the weave of life's embrace,
Lose the fear that holds the thread,
Find the beauty, find your place,
On this path where angels tread.

Forgotten Footsteps on Sacred Earth

In the quiet of the morn,
Forgotten trails softly lie,
Echoes of lives once sworn,
To tread lightly, never die.

Leaves may whisper ancient tales,
Roots entwined in sacred soil,
Through the storms and autumn gales,
Resilience borne from gentle toil.

In the grass, old footprints fade,
Yet each step, a promise made,
Through the seasons, love displayed,
In the heart, true paths are laid.

Nature cradles every prayer,
With every heartbeat, every breath,
In the stillness, we declare,
Life renews, even in death.

So we walk, with heads held high,
Through forgotten paths we roam,
In our souls, we lift the sky,
Finding solace, we are home.

Celestial Blessings in Empty Spaces

In the silence of the night,
Stars whisper ancient light.
A kiss of grace from above,
Filling hearts with endless love.

Empty spaces hold the truth,
Where the spirit finds its proof.
In shadows bright, the light expands,
Guided by divine hands.

Every breath a sacred prayer,
Softly floating in the air.
Faith ignites the darkest hour,
Transcending time, a holy power.

Within stillness, peace resides,
In the void, the heart confides.
Celestial realms, vast and wide,
Embrace the soul that seeks to glide.

With open hearts, we seek the way,
Trusting in the dawn of day.
Celestial blessings freely flow,
In empty spaces, love will grow.

Gifts of the Frayed Heartstrings

From the depths of sorrow's wake,
Tender strings begin to break.
Yet in pain, a beauty beams,
Resilience woven through our dreams.

Each tear a jewel, shining bright,
Crafted in the darkest night.
Love's fabric holds the fray,
Strength emerges from the clay.

Embrace the wounds that never fade,
In their scars, our truths are laid.
Gifts of grace in shattered parts,
Frayed heartstrings unite our hearts.

Through the fractures, light can seep,
In our struggles, wisdom deep.
Every loss, a lesson gained,
In the heart's song, joy remains.

Open arms will welcome fate,
Beneath the burden, we sedate.
Gifts of the frayed heartstrings sing,
In harmony, our souls take wing.

Rest in the Surrendered Mind

In the chaos of the day,
Let thoughts gently fade away.
In surrender, find your peace,
Where the racing winds do cease.

Quiet whispers, soft and clear,
In stillness, God draws near.
Let go of the weight you bear,
In the void, a sacred prayer.

Rest your heart, and close your eyes,
In the depths, the spirit flies.
Mind released from worldly binds,
In surrender, true love finds.

Trust the journey, feel the grace,
In the quiet, find your place.
Surrendered minds should seek the light,
A tranquil heart in endless night.

Hold the moment, breathe it in,
In this stillness, peace begins.
Rest in the surrendered mind,
A tranquil joy that's hard to find.

The Dance of Release

In sacred rhythms, hearts align,
Let the burdens fall like wine.
Through the tempest, spirits soar,
In the dance, there lies the door.

Each step forward, leave the past,
In the present, shadows cast.
With each turn, find the embrace,
As we flow in time and space.

Release the ties that hold you tight,
In the movement, find your light.
Gently shedding what must go,
In the dance, our souls will glow.

Like the river's constant flow,
Letting go is wisdom's glow.
In every spin, a new release,
Find divinity in this peace.

Through the dance, we rise, we live,
In the letting, we forgive.
The dance of life, a sacred chance,
In the rhythm, we find romance.

Beneath the Weight of Reverence

In silence, hearts bow low,
Beneath the sky's vast glow.
Whispers of faith in the night,
Guide us to sacred light.

In shadows, we seek grace,
Finding love in every place.
With prayers like gentle streams,
We awaken holy dreams.

Each moment, a chance to stand,
With open hearts, hand in hand.
Through trials, our spirits rise,
Revealing the truth in our eyes.

A hymn flows deep within,
Carried forth by silent kin.
The soul's weight, lighter still,
In unity, we find our will.

Beneath the weight, we kneel,
Embracing the love we feel.
Together, we breathe the air,
Bound by faith, beyond despair.

The Sacred Art of Release

In the stillness of the dawn,
Let burdens gently be gone.
With each breath, we learn to let,
All the doubts we harbor yet.

Waves of peace begin to rise,
Caught within compassion's sighs.
Releasing chains that bind the heart,
Making space for a new start.

Like the leaves that turn to gold,
We embrace the stories told.
In surrender, find your song,
Where the spirits all belong.

With hands lifted to the sky,
Each prayer a soft goodbye.
We enter into sacred trust,
Transforming ash to holy dust.

The art of letting love flow,
Embracing the seeds we sow.
With every tear, a new birth,
In the cycle of this earth.

Wings of Surrendered Spirit

On winds of sacred grace,
We find our destined place.
With wings outstretched and pure,
In surrender, we endure.

Through storms that rise and fall,
Hearts united, we stand tall.
In the ebb and flow of fate,
Faith assures, it's never late.

As whispers guide the way,
We embrace the light of day.
With trust, we let it be,
Flowing like a river's spree.

The spirit's dance, divine and free,
Soars above the troubled sea.
Every heartbeat, a step taken,
In surrender, we're not shaken.

Through valleys dark and deep,
Hope within us, we shall keep.
With wings spread wide, we fly,
Toward the beauty of the sky.

Embracing the Divine Departure

In twilight's gentle embrace,
We gather in this holy space.
With gratitude that knows no end,
We honor what we cannot mend.

Each heartbeat, a whispered prayer,
In the stillness, we lay bare.
Releasing all that once was known,
In the grace of love, we've grown.

With every breath, a soft farewell,
To stories no longer to tell.
In the tender light we find,
Our spirits interlaced, aligned.

Life's journey, a winding road,
In silence, we share the load.
Embracing change, the sacred flow,
In letting go, our souls glow.

The divine whispers in the night,
Illuminating hearts with light.
In departure, we release,
Embracing love, embracing peace.

Reflections on the Journey Ahead

In shadows deep, our faith will grow,
The path is set, yet not quite clear.
Each step we take, the seeds we sow,
In search of grace, we cast our fear.

The mountains rise, the valleys fall,
A whisper calls, a guiding light.
Through trials faced, we heed the call,
With hearts alight, we find our sight.

In moments still, we gather strength,
The journey's load, together shared.
With every breath, we go the length,
In faith united, souls prepared.

As dawn breaks new, we rise to see,
The horizon gleams, a promise bright.
In every step, we find our glee,
To walk in love, and seek the right.

Through joys and pains, our spirits reach,
In unity, we find our song.
In love's embrace, we gently teach,
Together bound, where we belong.

Trusting the Celestial Flow

Beneath the stars, we find our place,
With faith as tides, our hearts afloat.
Though storms may rise, there's endless grace,
In cosmic dance, we learn to gloat.

Each moment spins, a thread so fine,
The universe, a grand design.
In every breath, the sacred sign,
To trust the flow, in faith we shine.

When doubts arise, we look within,
The light of love, our guiding star.
Through every loss, through every win,
We ride the waves, no matter how far.

In silence deep, we hear the call,
The rhythm of the spheres above.
In every rise, in every fall,
We find our peace, we find our love.

So let our hearts be open wide,
Embracing all that life can show.
With spirit strong, and arms spread wide,
We trust the path, the sacred flow.

A Heart Prepared for Change

With courage firm, we stand today,
Embracing all that life may bring.
The winds of change sweep hopes away,
Yet deep within, our spirits sing.

The lessons learned, like gentle rain,
Will nourish growth in barren lands.
In trust, we rise from every pain,
With open hearts, we make our stands.

As seasons shift, we flow with grace,
A dance of life, both wild and pure.
In every trial, we find our place,
With faith anew, our hearts endure.

The door swings wide, the future calls,
A path unseen, yet brightly shines.
We gather strength as darkness falls,
For love's embrace, our heart defines.

In harmony, we seek the light,
With every change, our spirits grow.
As stars surround this wondrous night,
We walk with joy, prepared to flow.

The Stillness of Unraveled Threads

In quietude, we find our peace,
As life unravels, we stand still.
Each tangled thread is sweet release,
With every breath, we feel the thrill.

Among the chaos, beauty glows,
In tender hearts, the stillness swells.
With faith as compass, wisdom flows,
Where love abides, our spirit dwells.

The tapestry of life unfolds,
In every fray, a story spun.
A myriad of truths and folds,
In darkness met, the light begun.

In gentle hands, we weave our dreams,
Through trials passed, the bonds we bind.
In silence deep, our laughter beams,
As love unites, and hearts aligned.

So let us pause, and breathe in time,
With faith our guide, we find what's true.
For in this stillness, hearts will climb,
To weave the world in love anew.

Faithful Hand in the Letting Slip

In the silence of the night, we sigh,
A faithful hand reaches to the sky.
Letting slip the burdens that we bear,
Trusting in the love that lingers there.

Each moment drifts like grains of sand,
We find our solace in His gentle hand.
Though shadows loom and doubts may rise,
We walk on paths of truth, so wise.

In the letting go, our hearts grow light,
For in surrender, we find the might.
With faith as our compass through the fray,
We cling to hope that guides our way.

Every tear that falls is not in vain,
In every struggle, there's a holy gain.
For in the letting slip, we find our song,
A melody of grace, where we belong.

So let us raise our voices high,
To the skies that stretch like an endless tie.
In the faithful hand, we take our stand,
And trust in the love, forever planned.

Clutching Light Amongst the Shadows

Amidst the shadows that dance and play,
We clutch to light that guides our way.
In the heart of darkness, a flicker ignites,
A beacon of hope on the coldest nights.

With every step on this winding road,
We carry our burdens, we shoulder the load.
Yet in the trials, His love remains,
A whisper of comfort amidst our pains.

Clutching the light that shines so bright,
We find our courage to face the fight.
For in the depths of despair we stand,
With faith unyielding, we take His hand.

The shadows may twist and loom so near,
But in our hearts, He casts out fear.
In every struggle, our spirits rise,
As we seek the truth beyond the lies.

Together we journey, hand in hand,
Clutching the light, we make our stand.
In faith and love, we break the night,
For hope resounds in the clutching light.

Chosen to Wander, Blessed to Part

In the wilderness where the pathways meet,
We find the grace beneath our feet.
Chosen to wander and roam afar,
With hearts ignited by a guiding star.

Paths diverge in the twilight glow,
Yet in our souls, His light will flow.
For every journey has its end,
In the blessed parting, we transcend.

With open arms, we embrace the calls,
To venture out beyond the walls.
For every blessing, a tender chance,
In the dance of life, we learn to prance.

Though separations may bring us sorrow,
We hold the hope of a brighter tomorrow.
Blessed to part, we grow in grace,
To carry each memory in our embrace.

So let us wander, unafraid to explore,
For in every step, there's so much more.
Chosen to wander, we find our heart,
In the sacred journey, we play our part.

The Altar of What Was

At the altar where our memories lie,
We gather moments that whisper goodbye.
What once was laughter now offers peace,
In the stillness, our wounds find release.

With every echo, a story unfolds,
The past, a treasure, with blessings untold.
We kneel before the altar of time,
To honor the journey, each reason, each rhyme.

Though hearts may ache for the days gone by,
We see the beauty in the tears we cry.
For in each farewell, there's a sacred bond,
A love that lingers and goes beyond.

We kindle the flame of what shaped our fate,
In gratitude, we celebrate.
At the altar, our spirits revive,
For in the letting go, we truly thrive.

So here we stand, in the light of dawn,
With hopes renewed, we carry on.
At the altar of what was, we set free,
The past that shapes our destiny.

The Beauty Found in Letting Go

In the quiet night, we release our chains,
A soft whisper carries, through storm and through rain.
Fears fade like shadows in the dawning light,
In surrender, we find our souls take flight.

Letting go of burdens, we embrace the peace,
From the ashes of struggle, a new heart's lease.
Love blooms in the spaces where we once held tight,
In the warmth of forgiveness, our spirits ignite.

The past may linger like a fleeting ghost,
Yet, in each lost moment, we find what we boast.
In the beauty of trust, we allow to be,
A dance of the spirit, set finally free.

With hands open wide, we welcome the change,
In the tapestry woven, our lives rearrange.
Each tear we have fallen, each joy that we've known,
Builds a bridge to the heavens, where we are all shown.

Letting go unbinds us, from sorrowful ties,
In the grace of acceptance, our heart truly flies.
With every farewell, a new dawn will rise,
In the beauty of letting go, love multiplies.

Hushed Voices in the Realm of Goodbye

In the stillness of dusk, we whisper farewell,
To the dreams that we held, in our heart's sacred well.
Each word lightly spoken, like petals on air,
Echoes in silence, a sorrow we share.

Hushed voices linger in the tapestry's seams,
As we part from the places that cradled our dreams.
In the softness of twilight, memories dance,
With each tender glance, a bittersweet chance.

Through shadows and echoes, our spirits ascend,
In the realm of goodbye, old wounds find their mend.
Though paths may diverge, love's light shall remain,
In the heart's quiet chambers, through joy and through pain.

Grains of sand slipping through fingers so light,
Each moment a blessing, in the fading light.
With every soft goodbye, a promise resounds,
In the hush of the evening, eternal love found.

Though goodbyes may linger, with bittersweet grace,
In the whispers of heaven, our souls find their place.
With hushed, sacred voices, we carry our song,
In the realm of goodbye, we forever belong.

A Song for the Unbound Spirit.

Awake in the dawn, the spirit takes flight,
With wings made of dreams, it soars to the light.
Each note of creation, a melody pure,
In the song of the cosmos, our hearts find their cure.

The river of life flows, unbroken, divine,
In harmony's embrace, we find the sublime.
With every small flutter, the heart starts to sing,
In the choir of freedom, we feel the love spring.

Let the winds of the earth guide your way through,
In the dance of the heavens, find the essence of you.
With laughter like raindrops, joy spreads across skies,
In the song of the unbound, existence replies.

Through valleys of sorrow and mountains of grace,
The spirit unravels, revealing our place.
In the cadence of life, every heartbeat a prayer,
The unbound song whispers, transcending despair.

Join hands with the cosmos, in each breath we take,
A reverence for living, for love's gentle wake.
In the song of the unbound, we rise and we flow,
As one with the universe, forever we know.

Beneath the Sacred Sky

Underneath the sacred sky, we stand in awe,
The universe whispers, its beauty a law.
Stars twinkle softly, like jewels in the night,
Guiding our journey, with their tender light.

In the stillness of nature, we hear the call,
Every leaf and each breeze shares wisdom to all.
With hearts intertwined, we seek to explore,
The depths of creation, its endless shore.

Mountains rise proudly, with stories to tell,
Of struggles and triumphs, like echoes that swell.
Beneath the vast heavens, our spirits unite,
In the glow of creation, we find pure delight.

As sun paints the horizon with colors so bright,
We awaken to love in the soft morning light.
In the shadows of doubt, faith lights our way,
Beneath the sacred sky, we forever stay.

With every new dawn, hope rises anew,
In the dance of existence, we cherish the view.
Through valleys and peaks, with courage we fly,
Forever embraced, beneath the sacred sky.

The Covenant of Letting Go

In shadows deep, we find our way,
With whispered grace, we learn to sway.
Releasing chains that bind our soul,
In faith we trust, we become whole.

The dawn will rise, a gentle light,
To guide our hearts throughout the night.
With every breath, we shed the weight,
In surrender, we choose our fate.

Let go of fears, embrace the pure,
In the silence, we find the cure.
With open arms, the promise calls,
In faith we rise, though darkness falls.

The past is but a fleeting sigh,
In love's embrace, we learn to fly.
With spirits high, we walk the path,
In harmony, we find the math.

The Covenant speaks of trust and grace,
In every heart, in every place.
As we let go, we find our song,
In unity, we all belong.

A Divine Interlude of Change

In the stillness, a voice is heard,
Whispering hope, a sacred word.
With every shift, we walk anew,
In heaven's light, we find the view.

The seasons turn, the tides do shift,
In every change, we find the gift.
As petals fall, new blooms arise,
In life's grand dance, our spirits rise.

A gentle breeze, a calming sound,
In nature's pulse, love can be found.
With open hearts, we greet the shift,
In every challenge, find the lift.

The path ahead may twist and bend,
With each new dawn, our hearts extend.
Embrace the change, let fears subside,
In trust we walk, with God as guide.

A divine interlude, we embrace,
In love's rhythm, we find our place.
With every breath, shed doubt and pain,
In hope reborn, we rise again.

Sacred Farewell to the Past

With bows of grace, we bid adieu,
To shadows cast and dreams untrue.
The echoes fade, yet wisdom stays,
In lessons learned, we find our ways.

Each step we take, a vow to heal,
In memories cherished, love we feel.
The past, a bridge to what's ahead,
In gratitude, we shall be led.

The sands of time, they slip away,
In every heartbeat, night and day.
With gentle hands, we clasp the light,
In love's embrace, we take our flight.

The sacred vow, we honor still,
A journey onward, bound by will.
With open hearts, we pave the road,
In faith we walk, our spirits glowed.

A farewell whispered, soft and pure,
With every tear, our souls secure.
In healing grace, we find the peace,
In love's embrace, our hearts release.

The Quietude of Unbinding Hearts

In silence deep, we find our space,
Where love resides, a warm embrace.
With tender hands, we unbind fears,
In sacred trust, we dry our tears.

The quietude, a gentle balm,
In stillness found, our hearts are calm.
Through whispered prayers, our spirits soar,
In sacred unity, we restore.

Let go the burdens we both bear,
In letting in the softest air.
With every breath, our souls renew,
In love's embrace, we find what's true.

The moments shared, both sweet and clear,
In the silence, we draw near.
With open hearts, we weave the thread,
In every word, the love is spread.

The quietude holds sacred space,
In every heartbeat, find our grace.
With unbinding love, we start to see,
In life's pure dance, we come to be.

Heavenly Whispers of Farewell

In silent night, the angels call,
A gentle breeze, a soft enthrall.
With heavy hearts, we bid adieu,
Heavenly whispers, ever true.

In shimmering light, the path is clear,
Beyond the veil, we cast our fear.
With every breath, a sacred prayer,
In love we rise, into the air.

As stars align, we find our peace,
In dawn's embrace, our souls release.
With tender grace, the journey starts,
Together still, though miles apart.

The echoes fade, but never cease,
In hearts that hold, eternal lease.
With every tear, a bond renewed,
In whispered love, we shall pursue.

A final wave, a sweet goodbye,
In faith we stand, beneath the sky.
For in the night, their voices sing,
A lullaby, on angel's wing.

The Light Beyond the Horizon

As dawn breaks soft, the world awakes,
A promise made, as morning shakes.
With eyes upturned, we seek the light,
That guides our souls through endless night.

In every heart, a spark divine,
A burning hope, a love that shines.
Through trials faced, we hold the flame,
In sacred trust, we speak His name.

Across the hills, the angels soar,
In golden hues, they softly roar.
A call to arms, to brave the fight,
With every step, we claim our right.

Through winding paths, the shadows grow,
Yet in our hearts, the courage flows.
In unity, we stand as one,
Embracing grace, till day is done.

Beyond the mist, a radiant hue,
In love's embrace, we rest anew.
For in the light, our spirits blend,
In timeless peace, we find our end.

Graced by the Hands of Time

In gentle hands, the moments rest,
Each tick a gift, a sacred quest.
Woven paths of joy and strife,
In every breath, the breath of life.

Through seasons change, the heart expands,
In quiet times, we understand.
With every trial, a lesson shared,
In love's embrace, we are prepared.

The sands of time, they slip away,
Yet promise shines, a bright array.
Each memory, a precious stone,
In the tapestry, we're not alone.

As twilight falls, the shadows blend,
In whispered dreams, we make amends.
With gratitude, we lift our eyes,
To stars that twinkle in the skies.

For every heartbeat shares a truth,
In grace bestowed, we find our youth.
With every dawn, new chances rise,
In love eternal, our spirits fly.

A Pilgrim's Release

With weary feet, the journey long,
In search of peace, we sing our song.
Through valleys low and mountains high,
In faith, we wander, never shy.

The road unfolds, a path unknown,
Each step a seed, a prayer sown.
In every tear, a strength regained,
In barren lands, our hope remained.

The sunset paints the sky in gold,
With whispered tales of love retold.
In journeys past, we find our way,
In every night, awaits the day.

As time draws near, the heart takes flight,
To realms unseen, beyond our sight.
In grace we trust, our spirits soar,
In endless love, we are restored.

With open arms, we stand as one,
In sacred space, our souls have won.
As pilgrims bold, our hearts set free,
In light divine, eternally.

Serene Pathways to Freedom

In whispers soft, the spirits call,
To tread the path so wide and tall.
Each step unveils a truth so pure,
In freedom's light, our hearts endure.

The gentle breeze, a holy song,
It guides the weary, makes them strong.
With open hearts, we seek the way,
To leave behind our doubts and fray.

Through fields of gold, we wander free,
In nature's grace, our souls agree.
Embrace the love, let shadows fade,
On serene pathways, unafraid.

Beneath the stars, we find our peace,
In silent moments, worries cease.
The journey blooms in sacred space,
Where every heartbeat finds its grace.

Together we walk, hand in hand,
In faith we trust, a promised land.
Let joy arise, let sorrows bow,
In freedom's name, we live right now.

Sacred Trust in Letting Go

In gentle hands, we place our fear,
To trust the light that draws us near.
With every breath, we start anew,
In sacred trust, our spirits grew.

Release the weight, let burdens sleep,
In letting go, the soul finds leap.
A tapestry of love unfolds,
In freedom found, our hearts behold.

With open palms, we cast aside,
The chains that once our hearts did hide.
Embrace the flow, let currents guide,
In sacred trust, our souls abide.

Each moment's gift is ours to claim,
In letting go, we fan the flame.
A fire ignited, shining bright,
In unity, we find our light.

Together in this dance of night,
We honor pain, we seek the light.
In sacred trust, we rise and sing,
The symphony of hope we bring.

The Burden of Unfound Chains

In deepest woods, where shadows dwell,
The heart may ache, the spirit swell.
Yet chains unseen can bind us tight,
In darkness we must search for light.

In whispered fears, the doubt may grow,
Yet strength resides in seeds we sow.
The journey calls, though paths may twist,
To find the truth, we must persist.

Take heart, dear soul, from pain arise,
In every wound, a chance to rise.
The burden lifts when love is sought,
With open arms, peace is wrought.

Through trials faced, we learn to see,
The chains are only thoughts that flee.
In faith we stand, prepared to break,
To claim the life we long to make.

So cast aside what dims the flame,
Embrace your spirit, call your name.
In finding strength, we break the binds,
The burden fades, our heart unwinds.

Prayerful Letting Drift Away

In prayerful murmurs, softly spoken,
We gather dreams of hearts unbroken.
With every sigh, we let them fly,
To heavenly realms where spirits cry.

The burdens shared in sacred trust,
Transform our pain, return to dust.
In stillness lies the strength to part,
A whispered prayer, a hopeful heart.

With faith, we cast our worries low,
In gentle tides, we learn to flow.
As leaves release from autumn trees,
We find our peace in every breeze.

Each tear a river, pure and vast,
In letting drift, we honor past.
The weight we shed, a sacred gift,
In prayerful letting, hearts will lift.

So close your eyes, let silence speak,
In trust, you find the strength you seek.
In every prayer, the soul draws near,
To joy that blooms when love is clear.

Crafting Freedom in Holy Silence

In solitude, the heart does sing,
Where whispers rise on angel's wing.
Through stillness found, our spirits soar,
Unlocking chains, forevermore.

With gentle grace, we seek the calm,
A place where chaos meets the balm.
The quietude, a sacred art,
In holy silence, we depart.

The soul's reflection in the night,
Crafts paths of freedom, pure and bright.
In every breath, a chance to mold,
Through silence, stories yet untold.

As shadows fade, the truth prevails,
In tranquil moments, love exhales.
With every pause, a prayer ignites,
Crafting freedom in purest lights.

A Prayer for the Wrenched Heart

O Lord, hear this humble plea,
For those who ache, and long to be free.
Through trials deep, and sorrow's wail,
Wrap them close, let love prevail.

A wrenched heart seeks solace true,
In every tear, a strength anew.
Like petals wilted, yet so divine,
Restore the spirit, let hope align.

With tender hands, mend what is torn,
A healing light, when we are worn.
In shadows cast, let mercy gleam,
A prayer for hearts that yearn and dream.

May whispers of grace gently flow,
As burdens lift, and peace bestow.
For every sorrow, bring forth delight,
A prayer for the wrenched heart, shining bright.

Illuminated by the Light of Absence

In the quiet, shadows reside,
Absence speaks where hearts collide.
Yet in the dark, a glow remains,
Illuminating love's refrains.

Learning to dance with what is lost,
Embracing stillness, counting the cost.
For every void, a lesson grows,
In absence, spirit's essence flows.

The echoes of laughter softly fade,
Yet memories linger, never betrayed.
In light of absence, hope is born,
A journey through love, weathered and worn.

With every tear, a star ignites,
Guiding us through the longest nights.
Illuminated by that sacred space,
Where absence weaves a tender grace.

The Sacred Breath of Letting Go

In every exhale, find release,
A sacred breath, a path to peace.
As mountains bow to flowing streams,
Letting go births new dreams.

With open hands, we learn to trust,
In shifting sands, the soul is dust.
To let it be, to simply flow,
The sacred breath of letting go.

Each moment whispers, urging change,
Embracing life, though it feels strange.
In solitude, with heart aglow,
We find the strength in letting go.

A dance of grace, through ebb and flow,
Letting shadows rest, let light bestow.
Through sacred breath, we rise and soar,
In the art of faith, forevermore.

Solace in the Silent Night

In the quiet of the night, we pray,
For peace to guide our weary way.
Stars above, like angels, shine,
Whispers of love from the divine.

Heartbeats echo in the still,
Trusting in the sacred will.
Moonlight glows on paths we tread,
Gracing dreams and hopes unsaid.

In shadows deep, our fears take flight,
Held by faith, dispelling fright.
With every sigh, we find our song,
In solitude, we all belong.

Cloaked in night, the spirit soars,
Finding peace behind closed doors.
Each breath a promise, born anew,
In silence, our hearts pursue.

From the darkness, we arise,
Glimmers of hope illuminate the skies.
In quietude, we come to see,
The grace that always sets us free.

Embraced by the Divine Breeze

Gentle winds caress the trees,
Whispers of love in the evening's ease.
Nature sings in harmony,
Each note a prayer, eternally.

The daylight fades, the stars unite,
In breaths of warmth, pure and bright.
Every rustle tells a tale,
Of faith undying, that will prevail.

In the air, a sacred song,
Calling us where we belong.
Embraced by whispers of the night,
Each moment crafted, pure delight.

Clouds drift softly, hearts entwined,
In the breeze, our souls aligned.
With every gust, we find our peace,
In nature's beauty, worries cease.

Through the dusk, a light appears,
Wiping clean our hidden fears.
In every breath, the spirit roams,
Connected always, we are home.

Blossoms of Forgotten Hopes

In the garden where dreams fade,
Silent wishes lay unmade.
Petals fall like tears from grace,
Yet in the heart, they find their place.

As seasons change, we stand and wait,
For sunlit joy to meet our fate.
In every bud, the promise grows,
Resilience blooms where love bestows.

From ashes rise the flowers bright,
Illuminating the darkest night.
Each colorful burst, a sacred vow,
To nurture hope, here and now.

Fragile yet fierce, the blooms awake,
Their beauty all the heart can take.
And in their fragrance, memories dance,
Whispers of faith in every chance.

Though hopes once lost may seem far gone,
In every seed, life carries on.
For even in shadows, blossoms thrive,
Reminding us that dreams survive.

Rivers of Resilience

Flowing waters tell a tale,
Of trials faced and hearts that sail.
Each twist and turn a lesson learned,
In the depths, the fire burned.

Rivers winding through the land,
Carrying dreams, both bold and grand.
With every current, strength anew,
A testament to what we do.

Storms may rage, and shadows loom,
Yet through the struggle, flowers bloom.
Against the rocks, we carve our way,
In the river's flow, we choose to stay.

From mountains high to valleys low,
In sacred waters, courage flows.
Each ripple sings of hope's embrace,
In life's vast journey, we find grace.

So let us ride these waves with pride,
With faith as our ever-present guide.
For in the rivers wild and free,
Lives the power of unity.

The Graceful Exit of Love

In twilight's glow, love softly fades,
A whispering breeze, the heart invades.
With every sigh, a echo is found,
In silence, our lost dreams resound.

As stars emerge from the evening's crest,
We hold our truth, our souls at rest.
Each tear, a blessing, a journey's thread,
In love's embrace, our fears are shed.

Through shadows cast, a light remains,
In memories rich, love sustains.
A gentle path, we tread with grace,
In every parting, find a place.

Though we may walk on different shores,
In spirit's dance, our hearts explore.
The grace of love, in whispers thick,
Awaits us all, as time ticks.

Let not the sorrow weigh too deep,
In fate's kind hand, our laughter keep.
For love won't die, nor vanished be,
In the corners of eternity.

Hearts Alight in Farewell

As sunlight wanes, our hearts ignite,
A flame of love, in soft twilight.
With every glance, our worlds we share,
In gentle whispers, a sacred prayer.

In parting moments, the echoes play,
A melody sweet, that won't decay.
Each heartbeat pulses, a vibrant sound,
In the dance of grace, our souls unbound.

Through trials faced, and storms we braved,
In love's embrace, our spirits saved.
Though paths may shift, and roads divide,
In memories rich, our hearts abide.

With every tear, a story told,
In colors bright, our love unfolds.
Embrace the night, and let it be,
For farewell holds, eternity.

As stars ignite in the vast unknown,
In the heart's chamber, we are never alone.
For in each farewell, a kiss of fate,
A promise kept, we shall await.

The Humble Pilgrimage Away

A journey starts with a single step,
In quiet faith, our hearts adept.
With each ascent, the burdens shed,
On paths of grace, our spirits led.

Through valleys low, and mountains high,
We seek the truth, beneath the sky.
With open hands, we walk the line,
In humble prayer, our souls align.

As seasons change and rivers flow,
The love we share continues to grow.
In every moment, no step in vain,
In life's embrace, we break the chain.

Though trials test, and storms may rage,
In the book of life, we turn the page.
With faith as compass, we roam free,
In every heart, a sacred decree.

So take the road and don't delay,
In the humble pilgrimage, find your way.
For every path leads to the light,
In love's sweet journey, all is right.

Blessings Born from Release

In autumn's breath, the leaves let go,
A dance of change, in softest flow.
With every parting, a yield to grace,
In love's embrace, we find our place.

Through heartache's door, new life breaks through,
A gentle shift, a sky so blue.
From shards of pain, the bloom reveals,
The strength we hold, our spirit heals.

For blessings rise from what we free,
In letting go, we truly see.
With open hearts, embrace the dawn,
In sacred trust, we carry on.

Though chains may bind, and shadows loom,
In the warmth of love, we find our room.
In every sigh, a prayer takes flight,
Transforming dark to purest light.

So release the past, allow it to soar,
In every ending, there's so much more.
For blessings born from the pain we face,
Become the seeds of love and grace.

The Unseen Gift of Release

In the stillness of the night, we pray,
Let burdens lift, and fears decay.
With hands held high, we seek the grace,
In surrender, we find our place.

The chains of doubt begin to fall,
In release, we hear the call.
Whispers of love surround our heart,
A new beginning, a brand new start.

With every tear, a river flows,
In vulnerability, the spirit grows.
We unearth treasures hidden deep,
In faith's embrace, our souls shall leap.

Each sigh a song, each breath a prayer,
In letting go, we learn to care.
The unseen hand guides our way,
In the dance of night and day.

So, cast your burdens to the sky,
In the act of faith, we learn to fly.
The unseen gift is ours to hold,
In the warmth of love, we are consoled.

Emptiness as a Sacred Space

In the hollow of the heart, we find,
A sacred space, divinely kind.
Emptiness holds the promise clear,
A quiet voice, for those who hear.

Upon the altar of the soul,
Each void reveals a hidden whole.
In stillness, the spirit learns to soar,
Through emptiness, we explore.

Like a canvas untouched by paint,
In silence, we become the saint.
A sacred breath, a moment's pause,
In the void, we find the cause.

The echo of creation's song,
In emptiness, we all belong.
With open hearts, we dare to tread,
In the empty space, faith is fed.

So cherish the void, for therein lies,
The seeds of peace, a bright sunrise.
In emptiness, the spirit wakes,
To love's embrace, the heart partakes.

Embracing the Unknown

In shadows deep, the path unfolds,
With faith as guide, we break the molds.
Each step uncertain, yet divinely planned,
In the unknown, we take our stand.

The horizon whispers of untold grace,
A journey forward, a sacred space.
In mystery wrapped, our hearts ignite,
Embracing the dark, we seek the light.

With every heartbeat, we learn to trust,
In the dance of life, it's a must.
The unknown is not a place to fear,
But a doorway wide, to dreams so clear.

Through trials faced, our spirits grow,
In every doubt, new seeds we sow.
With hands outstretched, we greet the night,
Embracing the unknown, we find our light.

So take the leap, let your heart soar,
In the realm of faith, there is so much more.
For in the unknown, we find our song,
With love as our anchor, we are strong.

Found in the Shattered Silence

In the broken shards of silence sweet,
We gather grace at Jesus' feet.
Each fragment tells a story dear,
Of hope reborn, and faith sincere.

In quiet moments, we discover might,
Within the shadows, shines the light.
From shattered dreams, our spirits mend,
In silence deep, we find a friend.

With every pause, a breath of peace,
In shattered silence, fears release.
The heart's refrain, a gentle sound,
In stillness, sacred truth is found.

The noise of life fades far away,
In the shattered silence, we choose to stay.
With open hearts, we dare to see,
The beauty wrapped in mystery.

So listen closely, hear the song,
In shattered silence, we belong.
For in the cracks, life blooms anew,
With love as our guide, we're always true.

Echoes of Promise in the Void

In the silence, whispers flow,
Through the darkness, faith does grow.
Stars align, their light bestowed,
Guiding hearts on paths untold.

Hope remains, a soft caress,
In the night, a sweet recess.
Every tear, a sacred choice,
Echoes rise, we hear His voice.

Hands uplifted, prayers ascend,
In the void, His love shall mend.
Countless trials, yet we stand,
Held within His gentle hand.

From the depths, our spirits soar,
Drawing strength from ancient lore.
In His presence, fears dissolve,
A promise made, we shall evolve.

Through the shadows, light appears,
Washing away all doubts and fears.
With each step, our hearts confirm,
In His grace, we brightly turn.

A Journey Beyond the Grasp

Across the seas of time we sail,
Guided by the sacred tale.
Mountains rise, horizons bend,
In His arms, we find our friend.

Every heartbeat, a sacred trust,
In the journey, hope is just.
Paths unseen, yet souls are drawn,
In the twilight, we are reborn.

Through the valleys, shadows cast,
Forward, ever, we hold fast.
With each tear, a lesson learned,
In His light, our spirits burned.

Eagles soaring in the sky,
Lifted high, we cannot lie.
Strength renewed, we rise with grace,
In this journey, we find our place.

At the end, with arms outstretched,
Love awaits, our hearts refreshed.
Beyond the grasp, we find our home,
In His love, no more to roam.

When Dawn Sings of Release

Morning breaks, a soft embrace,
In the light, we find our place.
Shadows fade, the past released,
In the dawn, our spirits feast.

With each ray, a promise pure,
Healing hearts, forever sure.
Every burden, dropped in trust,
With His grace, we rise from dust.

Winds of change, they blow so sweet,
Leading us to hope's heartbeat.
Voices rise as stitches mend,
In His love, all wounds transcend.

When the sun paints skies anew,
Whispers of the heart break through.
For each sorrow, joy appears,
In His mercy, calm our fears.

As the world in silence wakes,
In remembrance, our spirit shakes.
When dawn sings, we shall embrace,
The freedom found in endless grace.

The Covenant of Unheld Dreams

In the night, our dreams take flight,
Bound by faith, we seek the light.
Every vision, etched in time,
In His heart, they truly shine.

Promises made in quiet prayer,
In the shadows, He is there.
Every whisper, a gentle call,
In His love, we shall not fall.

History speaks with sacred words,
Songs of hope like fluttering birds.
In the covenant, we arise,
Faithful hearts reach for the skies.

Unheld dreams, yet we aspire,
Fueling souls with holy fire.
In the silence, purpose blooms,
Guided by what love resumes.

As the stars twinkle above,
We are cradled in His love.
For every dream, a path unfolds,
In His kingdom, truth beholds.

A Symphony of Departing Souls

In shadows deep, where whispers dwell,
The souls ascend, we bid farewell.
With echoes sweet, their hymns arise,
A melody beneath the skies.

Transcending pain, they soar so high,
To realms where love shall never die.
In unity, their spirits flow,
A symphony of light aglow.

The gentle touch of grace surrounds,
In silence, truth within us sounds.
Each heartbeat sings of lost embrace,
In sacred space, we find our place.

Through veils of time, their voices call,
In every tear, we stand up tall.
With open hearts, we come anew,
In faith, the bond remains so true.

With every note, the past we weave,
In love's embrace, we shall believe.
A symphony that knows no end,
In light we stand, as soul and friend.

From Possession to Divine Belonging

In chains of want, our hearts entangle,
Yet deeper truths the soul can wrangle.
From earthly grasp, we rise to find,
A love that frees the weary mind.

As petals fall, the lessons bloom,
In sacrifice, we banish gloom.
From hollow dreams to sacred light,
We shift our gaze to love's true height.

In every loss, a seed is sown,
From barren ground, a tree has grown.
With open hands, we let it be,
Embracing what is meant to free.

Transcendent grace invites us near,
To share in joy, to conquer fear.
As echoes fade, we heed the call,
In letting go, we gain it all.

The path of faith, a sacred song,
Where every heart can learn to belong.
United in love, we're never lost,
In divine belonging, we find the cost.

Releasing the Chains of Mourning

In shadows cast, where silence weeps,
We gather close, our anguish deep.
Yet through the pain, a lesson gleams,
In every tear, the heart redeems.

With every sigh, we learn to breathe,
Releasing chains, in love, believe.
For in our grief, there lies a spark,
A light that shines within the dark.

The sacred dance of loss and gain,
In every heart, we bear the strain.
Yet through the veil of sorrow's night,
Rises the dawn, a day of light.

In memories sweet, they softly guide,
Through open doors, we shall not hide.
As phoenixes from ashes soar,
Our souls ascend, forevermore.

Through every wound, we find our song,
In love's embrace, we all belong.
With open hearts, we greet the morn,
In releasing chains, new hope is born.

Communion with the Unseen

In quietude, we seek the light,
Where whispers dwell in sacred night.
With open hearts, we tune our ears,
To ancient truths that calm our fears.

Beyond the veil, where spirits glide,
In unity, our souls abide.
With mindful breath, we bridge the space,
In silent prayer, we find our grace.

With realms unseen, our hearts align,
In every pulse, the divine shines.
The sacred comes, in whispers sweet,
In union pure, our spirits meet.

Through faith, we walk on sacred ground,
In gentle grace, our souls are found.
With every step, we find our kin,
In communion, we rise within.

In sacred stillness, love expands,
Embracing all with open hands.
The unseen world, a guiding light,
In love's embrace, the soul takes flight.

The Harvest of Letting Be

In fields of grace, we sow our tears,
Trusting the soil of passing years.
With hands released, we watch and wait,
The fruit of peace, a destined fate.

Through seasons' change, the spirits rise,
Each whispering wind, a soft surprise.
In silence grown, the heart can see,
The sacred yield of letting be.

Roots intertwine beneath the ground,
In gentle strength, our souls are bound.
The light above, so bright and clear,
Guides us where our truth appears.

As time unfolds, the heart will learn,
To cherish stillness, to discern.
In every grain, a lesson deep,
The harvest waits, the soul must reap.

Unfolding Beneath the Stars

Beneath the vast, eternal night,
We gather strength from ancient light.
Each twinkling spark, a story told,
Of dreams surrendered, hearts made bold.

In shadows cast by heavenly beams,
We find our path within the dreams.
Each moment shines, a gift bestowed,
To seekers on this winding road.

The cosmos whispers truths so rare,
In stillness found, a sacred prayer.
With every breath, the stars align,
Unfolding grace, divine design.

From dust to dawn, the journey flows,
In cosmic dance, our spirit grows.
In unity, we rise and gleam,
Unfolding hearts, a boundless dream.

The Faith to Forsake

With heavy heart, we stand and part,
A leap of faith, a brand new start.
Letting go of what once was bright,
Embracing shadows, seeking light.

In the quiet of the soul's deep night,
We find our way through fear and fright.
Each loss a lesson, each wound a gift,
In the letting go, our spirits lift.

With courage sown, we walk the path,
In every tear, the aftermath.
The promise of dawn, a soft embrace,
The faith to forsake, to find our place.

In the echoes of the past we hear,
A voice of hope that draws us near.
With every step, we learn to see,
The beauty born from letting be.

Harmony in the Unseen

In whispers soft, the spirit flows,
A symphony that gently grows.
Each note a breath, each pause a sigh,
In harmony, we learn to fly.

Beyond the veil, in realms of peace,
The unseen hands bring sweet release.
In trust we stand, in love reside,
Together in the spirit's tide.

As rivers merge and mountains bow,
We find the threads that weave our vow.
In unity, the soul will sing,
A dance of joy, in all we bring.

So let us weave in sacred space,
A tapestry of love and grace.
In harmony, the unseen bless,
The heart's embrace, our truest rest.

Releasing Sorrows to Celestial Winds

In the hush of twilight's glow,
Whispers rise where sorrows flow,
Casting burdens to the air,
Hearts alight with fervent prayer.

Let the winds take grief away,
Guiding thoughts, as night meets day,
In the stillness, peace descends,
A beginning as the sorrow ends.

With every tear that's gently shed,
Fleeting fears, like whispers, spread,
A soft release, an earning grace,
To find solace in love's embrace.

Hands raised high, to heavens plead,
In the face of doubt, take heed,
For in the void where pain resides,
Light emerges, where hope abides.

So we lift our voices, rise,
Like dawn breaking, beneath vast skies,
In this sacred, gentle sigh,
We surrender, let spirits fly.

A Testament to Timelessness

In the sacred halls of night,
Eons stretch, and stars ignite,
Each moment a whispering song,
Echoes of where we belong.

Ancient paths beneath our feet,
Timeless tales, where souls meet,
Fading shadows, yet they remain,
In our hearts, love's sweet refrain.

Between the dawn and dusk we stand,
Chasing dreams with earnest hands,
Every heartbeat a testament,
To the divine, a firm lament.

Through the ages, spirits flow,
With every joy, the seeds we sow,
In the tapestry of time and space,
We find the beauty in love's trace.

Voices whisper in the breeze,
Reminding us, we're all at ease,
For in the dance of endless dreams,
Life unfolds, or so it seems.

Holy Embrace of Parting

In the shadows where love departs,
Softly spoken, tender hearts,
Each farewell a sacred rite,
Lingering in the fading light.

Leaves falling, yet roots remain,
In each tear, a hint of pain,
But love's embrace does never fade,
In new paths, our hope is laid.

A gentle breeze, a whispered prayer,
In parting, we're forever aware,
Time's embrace, though brief and sweet,
Leads us on, where spirits meet.

Hold onto memories, bright and clear,
In every laugh, in every tear,
For love transcends the bounds of time,
In every note, a silent chime.

Thus we rise, though farewells sting,
With every sunset, new beginnings cling,
In this holy space, we trust,
A promise lies within the dust.

The Divine Dance of Ephemeral Things

In the dawn's blush, life unfolds,
Momentary, yet love upholds,
Each heartbeat a fleeting grace,
In the dance, we find our place.

Petals drift on gentle streams,
Chasing echoes of our dreams,
With every step, a spark divine,
In the sacred, we align.

Waves caress the golden shore,
Like laughter shared, forevermore,
Time's embrace, a loving tether,
In the now, we find forever.

Together we weave our fates anew,
Lost in colors, vast and true,
In the symphony of existence,
We discover love's persistence.

So let us twirl in joyous flight,
In the tapestry of day and night,
For every moment that slips away,
Is a note in life's grand ballet.

Spirit's Whisper in Empty Hands

In silence deep, the spirit sighs,
A gentle breath, where hope replies.
With empty hands, we seek the light,
Guided by faith, through darkest night.

The whispers echo, soft and clear,
In every heart, a voice we hear.
Though lacking riches, souls are rich,
In love's embrace, we find our niche.

The wind it carries sacred lore,
Of kindness vast, forevermore.
In every gesture, small yet grand,
The spirit lives, through empty hands.

A moment still, beneath the stars,
Reminds us all, we carry scars.
But through the pain, a bloom shall rise,
In every tear, a sweet surprise.

So listen close, to whispers fine,
Where every soul, seeks to align.
In empty hands, the world expands,
Embraced by grace, in sacred strands.

Contracts of the Soul Unraveled

In shadows cast, where truths abide,
The contracts made in spirits' tide.
With every choice, a path we weave,
In every heart, the power to believe.

The ink of fate on parchment worn,
A tale of trust, both bright and torn.
As bonds are forged, and vows entwine,
The dance of souls, divine design.

In the silence, questions rise,
Unraveling what's beneath the skies.
Each promise spoken, a sacred call,
In unity's grace, we rise, we fall.

The lessons learned, like incense burn,
In sacred cycles, our hearts discern.
To seek the truth within the pain,
Eternal growth, through joy and strain.

So break the chains, let spirits soar,
In contracts signed, we find much more.
For every end is but a start,
In union's bond, we heal the heart.

Benevolence in the Art of Departure

In every farewell, a lesson glows,
A bittersweet dance, where love still flows.
With open hearts, we say goodbye,
In every end, a chance to fly.

The art of leaving, always kind,
To cherish moments left behind.
Embrace the change, let sorrow wane,
In every loss, there's much to gain.

With gentle steps, we carve the way,
To honor those who cannot stay.
In every tear, a spark ignites,
Benevolence shines in darkest nights.

So lift your eyes, and trust the road,
For every burden is a load.
In every parting, blessings grow,
In love's embrace, we learn to flow.

To find the grace in letting go,
Is wisdom found in every soul.
For in the space where love departs,
Lies the foundation of our hearts.

Celestial Threads Unwound

In cosmic dance, we reach for stars,
Unraveling fate, through light and scars.
The threads of time, we weave anew,
In every moment, skies of blue.

With whispered prayers, the heavens call,
To touch the void, to rise, to fall.
Celestial hands, they guide our way,
In every dawn, a brand new day.

The universe sings a sacred song,
In harmony where we all belong.
Each thread unspooled, a story told,
In seraph's grace, our hearts behold.

So look above, and catch the gleam,
In every hope, a radiant dream.
For in the weave of life's great cloak,
Celestial love, forever spoke.

To dance among the stars so bright,
Is to embrace the source of light.
In every thread that's spun and twirled,
The fabric of our soul is curled.

Tidal Waves of Grace

In the stillness of the night, we pray,
Ebbing fears like tides away.
Grace descends like gentle rain,
Cleansing hearts, releasing pain.

In the morning light we rise,
With faith that stretches to the skies.
Waves of mercy, soft and pure,
In His love, we find our cure.

Through the storms that darken skies,
In His arms, we find the prize.
Hope is anchored, standing fast,
In the present, not the past.

Every wave's a sweet embrace,
Flowing forth, it fills the space.
Let the currents draw us near,
In His water, we have no fear.

As the ocean breathes and sighs,
Listen closely; hear our cries.
With each wave, His spirit flows,
In the depth, our purpose grows.

Hymns of the Unchained Spirit

Chains once held us, dark and cold,
But hearts set free, the truth be told.
With voices raised, we sing our praise,
In the light, we dwell always.

Mountains cannot block our way,
In the dawn, we find the day.
Hymns of joy, we lift them high,
As the heavens echo nigh.

Through valleys deep and shadows cast,
Faith ignites a light steadfast.
In unity, our hearts align,
Bound by love, divine design.

Each step forward, we reclaim,
In His name, we break all shame.
Chanting songs of hope and grace,
In His presence, we find our place.

Unchained spirits, bold and free,
Soaring high, eternally.
From the darkness, we take flight,
With the love that is our light.

In Solitude, We Find Our Peace

In the quiet of the morn,
Where the light of day is born,
In solitude, the spirit speaks,
With gentle whispers that it seeks.

Time alone, a sacred space,
Where we find His warm embrace.
In the silence, we discern,
Lessons of the heart we learn.

Meditation like a stream,
Flowing softly, pure as dream.
In our stillness, strength we find,
Calmly weaving heart and mind.

With every breath, we shed our strife,
In the stillness, breath of life.
Seeking truth in twilight's glow,
In solitude, our spirits grow.

Here the burdens lift away,
In His love, we choose to stay.
Among the shadows, peace we seek,
Finding solace when we're meek.

The Cost of Holding Too Tight

In the gripping of this life,
Holding close yet filled with strife.
Fingers clenched on fleeting things,
Bound by fear that burden brings.

Love demands a gentle hand,
To release and to understand.
Tightly held, the heart will break,
In the letting go, we wake.

Every bond must learn to bend,
In freedom lies, our truest friend.
As we clutch, the spirit aches,
In surrender, beauty wakes.

Wisdom whispers soft and low,
Letting go is how we grow.
In the balance, peace we'll find,
With open hearts and open minds.

So release what chains the soul,
Embrace the journey, seek the whole.
In the act of faith, we soar,
With love's embrace, we gain much more.

The Journey of Faithful Release

In shadows deep, the heart does seek,
A path of light, both pure and meek.
With every step, the burdens fade,
In trust we walk, His grace displayed.

The valleys low, the mountains high,
Through whispered prayers, we learn to fly.
Each doubt dissolves, like morning mist,
In faithful release, we find our bliss.

With open hands, we give our fears,
The journey calls, through joys and tears.
The spirit soars beyond the chains,
In love's embrace, true freedom reigns.

We follow stars that light the night,
In sacred peace, we find our sight.
With every heartbeat, we are free,
In faith we trust, eternally.

And when we reach the final shore,
We'll know in faith, we are much more.
For every step led us to grace,
In faithful release, our souls embrace.

An Offering to the Winds

Upon the breeze, our hopes we cast,
A whisper soft, a prayer amassed.
The winds of change, they guide our way,
In nature's song, we choose to stay.

With open hearts, we let love flow,
Each moment lived, seeds we sow.
To skies above, our voices rise,
An offering sweet, beneath the skies.

The rustling leaves, a sacred hymn,
In silence deep, we draw from Him.
Each breath a gift, each step a stride,
In unity, our hearts abide.

Through trials faced, our spirits grow,
In trust we stand, come rain or snow.
The winds will carry all we share,
An offering pure, a world laid bare.

Boundless the love that sweeps the land,
In nature's grace, we take our stand.
With every gust, our souls entwine,
An offering cherished, forever divine.

In the Shadow of Letting Go

In quiet hours, the shadows creep,
As memories linger, the heart weeps.
Yet in the dark, a light shall glow,
In the shadow, we learn to grow.

With every tear, a lesson learned,
In letting go, the soul has turned.
To trust the path, though unseen still,
In faith we walk, with steadfast will.

The weight we bear, we lay to rest,
In gentle hands, we are blessed.
Each moment passed, a step away,
In the shadow, we find the day.

With courage found in whispered sighs,
We rise anew, beneath the skies.
Though letting go may bring us fear,
In faith we find, the way is clear.

And when the dawn breaks, light will flow,
In the shadow of letting go.
Our spirits freed, like birds take flight,
In endless grace, we find our light.

Embracing the Dusk of Yesterday

In twilight's glow, we pause to see,
The echoes of what used to be.
With every dusk, a lesson learned,
In embracing time, our hearts discerned.

The faded dreams, like stars that fall,
In gentle whispers, we hear the call.
To cherish moments, both joy and strife,
In dusk's embrace, we find our life.

The shadows lengthen, but hope remains,
In every trial, a wisdom gains.
We honor all that has been lived,
In dusk's embrace, we learn to forgive.

With open arms, we greet the night,
For every ending brings new light.
In twilight's peace, the heart will mend,
Embracing the dusk, our journey blends.

Tomorrow waits with promise bold,
In every loss, a story told.
Embracing the dusk, we rise anew,
In faith and love, our vision true.

The Last Prayer of the Possessed

In shadows deep, the whispers cry,
A soul in torment, seeking the sky.
On bended knee, the spirit pleads,
Oh, grant me peace, fulfill my needs.

Chains of sorrow bind the night,
Yet flickers of hope ignite the light.
With trembling hands, I raise my voice,
In faith divine, I make my choice.

The weight of darkness, a heavy shroud,
Yet I stand firm, beneath the crowd.
In echoes lost, I seek the way,
To break the curse, to find the day.

With every breath, I hang in trust,
In sacred bond, my heart does rust.
Release my spirit, let it soar,
To realms of grace, forevermore.

In this last prayer, I know my fate,
For love and mercy shall not wait.
With open arms, I seek the light,
And leave behind the endless night.

Offering Up the Weight of Memory

In twilight's glow, the memories sigh,
Each fragment echoes, a tearful cry.
With hands outstretched, I offer up,
The weight of losses, the bitter cup.

Glimmers of joy and shadows of pain,
Entwined together like sun and rain.
I lay them softly upon the stone,
In sacred trust, no longer alone.

Through every trial, through every test,
I seek the truth, the heart's pure quest.
Oh, let me carry, let me bear,
The sacred tales, the silent prayer.

In whispered winds, the voices call,
Of those who've risen, who've faced the fall.
I hold their stories, like fragile seeds,
In fertile soil, where spirit leads.

Each memory cherished, each tear a gift,
In offering love, my spirits lift.
With open heart, I send them high,
To meet the stars, in endless sky.

Sacred Shadows of the Past

In the cloistered halls, shadows play,
Where whispers linger, night meets day.
Old echoes dance through ancient stone,
Each sigh a message, each breath a bone.

Through time-worn paths, the spirits tread,
Carving their truths where shadows spread.
In silent prayers, their voices rise,
To cradle the lost in gentle skies.

With every heartbeat, the past recedes,
Yet in its wake, the heart still bleeds.
In sacred silence, I seek to find,
The light within, the love aligned.

Each tear a lesson in love's embrace,
The sacred shadows, they leave their trace.
In holy stillness, I forge my way,
Through trails of hope, where spirits play.

So guide my heart, oh stars of old,
In stories woven, in dreams retold.
I anchor my soul to the skies of night,
In sacred shadows, I find my light.

Ghosts of the Heart Made Whole

Beneath the surface, they linger still,
The ghosts of love, the heart's own will.
In quiet moments, I hear their call,
Each echo a promise, never to fall.

In every heartbeat, a memory swells,
Of joy and sorrow, of love that dwells.
Their whispers guide me through darkened halls,
To find the strength when the silence falls.

Oh, holy specters, lost yet here,
In shadows cast, you bring me near.
With open arms, I embrace the pain,
For it is love that binds the chain.

Through every trial, through every tear,
The ghosts remind me that love is near.
In treasured moments, I seek the grace,
Of hearts made whole, in this sacred space.

So let me walk the paths of light,
With grateful heart, through day and night.
For in the ghosts, I find my way,
And celebrate life, come what may.

Silence in the Weight of the Past

In silence, whispers of yore,
Echo through the sacred door.
Each memory, a heavy stone,
Graced by light, yet all alone.

The shadows dance, they come and go,
Guiding hearts in ebb and flow.
Lessons learned in quiet sighs,
Transforming pain as hope does rise.

Beneath the shroud, the spirit knows,
A path towards where the river flows.
With faith as anchor, strong and fast,
We seek the peace that breaks the past.

In reverence, we bow and pray,
To find the strength to walk our way.
The weight will lift, the heart will soar,
In silent grace, we seek for more.

Embrace the echoes of the years,
Let every sorrow turn to tears.
For in the quietude, we find,
A solace deep, a love combined.

Anchored in Trusting Change

In winds of time, the seasons shift,
A constant call, a sacred gift.
With roots that deepen in the earth,
We stand in faith, and know our worth.

The river flows, it carves the stone,
Transforming all, and yet alone.
In each new dawn, there's hope to cling,
The heart of change, a sacred spring.

We are the vessels of His grace,
Navigating through time and space.
Embracing tides that come and go,
In surrender, we learn to grow.

When storms arise, our hearts may quake,
But trust the path, for truth's own sake.
With courage found in every plight,
We dance with shadows, seek the light.

The journey winds, yet we remain,
Anchored firm in love, through pain.
For change, a friend, will guide us still,
Towards valleys rich, and hearts to fill.

Stars Aligned for Letting Be

In twilight's glow, the stars unfold,
Stories written, bright and bold.
Each twinkle tells of journeys vast,
A universe in silence cast.

Beneath the heavens, hearts entwined,
Finding peace in what's been designed.
With every breath, we let them be,
In cosmic grace, our souls are free.

The dance of time, a rhythmic beat,
Guides us forward, bittersweet.
In letting go, we learn to trust,
Life's tender moments burst like dust.

With every star, a dream ignites,
Illuminating tranquil nights.
In the embrace of what we see,
We welcome all, and simply be.

A tapestry of light and shade,
In this vast sky, our fears do fade.
For as the stars begin to glow,
We find the truth in letting go.

The Essence of a Gentle Goodbye

In stillness felt, the heart prepares,
A moment cherished, love declares.
With whispered words and soft embrace,
We touch the soul, a sacred space.

The breeze will carry memories sweet,
As paths diverge, our hearts do meet.
With tears that fall like morning dew,
We find the strength to bid adieu.

In every sigh, a life well-lived,
A blend of loss and hope we give.
A gentle farewell, wrapped in grace,
To honor time and each warm place.

The journey onward calls us near,
With open hearts, we hold what's dear.
In parting ways, we bless the day,
In silence, love will always stay.

For every ending births a dawn,
In essence pure, we carry on.
With gentle goodbyes, we learn to see,
The beauty in all that cannot be.

The Embrace of Divine Dissolution

In shadows deep, the spirit sighs,
Awash in waves of sweet release.
Each breath a prayer, each tear a prize,
In Divine arms, I find my peace.

Let go the chains that bind the soul,
In sacred silence, I find my way.
As stars align to make me whole,
I know in darkness, light will stay.

The heart beats soft, a whispered hymn,
In every moment, grace abounds.
The world may fade, but love won't dim,
In stillness, endless joy resounds.

The veil of flesh begins to thin,
Transcending fears, I rise anew.
In losing self, I start to win,
Awake to all that is true.

In merging with the vast unknown,
I breathe the essence of the One.
In dissolution, I am home,
Forever bound, yet free to run.

The Quiet Joy of Departure

As dawn awakens with tender light,
The heart prepares to take its flight.
In silence sweet, the spirit glows,
Embraced by grace, it gently flows.

Each step is calm, each thought serene,
In letting go, the soul is seen.
The world behind fades softly gray,
While joy unfolds to lead the way.

A journey sweet, a path divine,
With every sigh, the stars align.
In quiet moments, wisdom speaks,
The promise of the peace we seek.

As shadows stretch and fade away,
A love eternal lights the day.
In this soft parting, I find trust,
In faith alone, I rise from dust.

The courage sprouts from tender grace,
With every heartbeat, I embrace.
In joyous flight, I see the dawn,
Through quiet joy, I carry on.

Lanterns Guiding the Wayward

In twilight's grace, the lanterns glow,
To guide the hearts that roam below.
With flickering light, they show the path,
In the still night, dispel the wrath.

Each soul a spark, a flicker's flame,
Yearning for love, yet playing a game.
In shadows deep, the light is near,
A whispered promise draws us here.

The wanderer's steps find solace sweet,
Each glowing orb beneath our feet.
In tangled thorns and winding ways,
The lanterns shine, our spirits raise.

As night unveils the hidden fears,
Each flicker holds the cries and tears.
Yet through the dark, we find our song,
Together as one, we all belong.

With open hearts, we trust the light,
In every storm, it shines so bright.
These lanterns, love, our guiding hand,
Together, we tread this sacred land.

Rising from Ashes

From ashes cold, the spirit wakes,
In every loss, the heart remakes.
The flames of change may burn so bold,
Yet from the heat, new dreams unfold.

In struggles faced, the courage grows,
Resilience found in ebb and flows.
With every trial, strength ignites,
And through despair, the soul takes flight.

In whispered prayers, the heart finds peace,
With every breath, the burdens cease.
Rising up high, the Phoenix soars,
Through storms of fate, the spirit roars.

The journey tough, yet love will lead,
In every step, the truth is freed.
From depths of darkness, light will sprout,
In union, there is no doubt.

Embrace the fire that burns inside,
In sacred trust, let love abide.
From ashes new, we find our place,
In life reborn, we see God's grace.

Adrift

In quiet waters, the spirit drifts,
Upon the waves, the heart uplifts.
Each moment's breath, a gentle plea,
In boundless seas, I long to be.

The currents pull in unknown ways,
With every turn, my heart obeys.
In searching dreams, the starry night,
A compass found in love's pure light.

Lost yet found, the depths embrace,
To feel the vastness of His grace.
In every doubt, a whisper speaks,
Through silent paths, my spirit seeks.

In drifting time, I learn to trust,
As waves crash down, in love I thrust.
In stillness deep, the storms dissolve,
Through faith, my soul begins to evolve.

Adrift in peace, I float and glide,
In every tide, my heart's my guide.
With open arms, I greet the dawn,
In faith, my journey carries on.

The Prayer of an Open Heart

In whispered tones, I seek Thy grace,
With every breath, I find my place.
Open my heart to love so pure,
In faith, my soul will ever endure.

Guide me through shadows, lead me home,
In Your embrace, I shall not roam.
Each step I take, let it be right,
Illuminate my path with holy light.

Lift me up where troubles lie,
With wings of hope, I learn to fly.
In prayer, I lay my burdens down,
Beneath Your watch, I will not drown.

Let kindness fill my every deed,
In every thought, let love be freed.
In listening silence, I shall hear,
The gentle voice that casts out fear.

Oh, grant me strength on this sweet road,
To share the light, to ease the load.
With open heart, I'll walk with Thee,
In faith's embrace, I feel so free.

Glimpses of What Lies Ahead

In prayerful stillness, visions bloom,
Of radiant paths beyond the gloom.
The horizon holds a sacred light,
Whispers of hope in the darkest night.

With each dawn, a promise unfurls,
New beginnings, as life twirls.
I glimpse the joy that time will weave,
In every struggle, I will believe.

Mountains rise, and valleys fall,
Through storm and trial, I hear Your call.
In every moment, Your truth I find,
A gentle guiding hand, so kind.

The future dances, wild and free,
With faith, I claim my destiny.
As stars ignite the velvet sky,
I stare in wonder, never shy.

O Lord, the years shall come and go,
Yet in my heart, Your love will grow.
These glimpses show what lies ahead,
In sacred trust, my spirit fed.

Unfurling Like Autumn Leaves

Like autumn leaves, I bend and sway,
In vibrant hues, I find my way.
Each moment's change, a work of art,
Unfurling grace, a brand new start.

The chill of night, a gentle cue,
To shed the past, embrace the new.
In surrender, there's strength to glean,
In every loss, Your love I've seen.

The branches ache but still reach high,
Connecting earth to the endless sky.
In every season, faith doesn't cease,
With every change, I find my peace.

With every rustle, whispers say,
"Breathe in the magic of today."
For in letting go, I truly gain,
The dance of life, joy mixed with pain.

Through cycles bright, I will abide,
In Nature's arms, where I confide.
Unfurling tender, like leaves in flight,
A testament to love's pure light.

A Testament to Freeing the Soul

With every heartbeat, truth reveals,
A testament of how love heals.
To break the chains that bind me tight,
And soar in freedom, pure and right.

From shadows deep, I rise anew,
Cleansed by tears, I see the true.
In every trial, a lesson learned,
Through fires of faith, my spirit burned.

The past may haunt, but it won't define,
I embrace the gift of the divine.
To live in peace, my ultimate quest,
In surrender, my soul finds rest.

With open arms, I greet the dawn,
In every moment, a new love drawn.
A fluttering heart, unchained and free,
In grace, I find my destiny.

O let me shine, Your light in me,
A testament of love's decree.
As I break free, forever bold,
With You, dear Lord, my heart behold.

In the Silence of Farewell

In stillness, we gather, hearts intertwined,
The echoes of love, gentle and blind.
We whisper our hopes to the stars above,
In the silence of parting, we cling to our love.

The dawn breaks softly, a new day will rise,
Yet shadows of memories linger in sighs.
Each tear that we shed, a testament true,
In the silence of farewell, I remember you.

Though paths may diverge, souls remain whole,
For love transcends time, it nurtures the soul.
In moments of doubt, a light will appear,
Guiding our hearts through the depths of our fear.

With faith as our anchor, we stand side by side,
Through valleys of sorrow and oceans of tide.
In the silence of farewell, may peace be our guide,
As we carry our love forever inside.

So let us embrace this sacred goodbye,
With gratitude deep, let our spirits fly.
In the silence of farewell, our souls will ignite,
In the warmth of its glow, we find love's light.

A Pilgrim's Path of Acceptance

On this journey of life, we wander and roam,
With footsteps of faith, we find our true home.
Each trial a lesson, each sorrow a sign,
In a pilgrim's path, we learn to divine.

Through mountains of doubt, we climb ever higher,
With hearts full of hope, igniting the fire.
We trust in the grace that each moment bestows,
On a pilgrim's path, acceptance just grows.

In whispers of nature, the Spirit does call,
Embracing the rise and embracing the fall.
With courage as armor, we bravely ascend,
On a pilgrim's path, we learn to transcend.

With each step we take, we surrender our pain,
In cycles of loss, there's a beauty to gain.
Through trials and triumphs, we come to know love,
On a pilgrim's path, guided from above.

So let us walk gently, with hearts open wide,
For each twist and turn is a gift from the tide.
On this journey together, may we ever stand tall,
In the grace of acceptance, we are one in it all.

The Grace in Fading Echoes

In twilight's soft glow, where shadows retreat,
Resounding the moments, both bitter and sweet.
The grace in the fading, we start to embrace,
As time weaves its story, we find our own place.

Each whisper of past, a lesson to heed,
In the garden of memories, we plant every seed.
For in what is lost, there's a beauty that grows,
With grace in fading echoes, our wisdom bestows.

In the silence, we hear the soft beating drum,
A rhythm of life, where we all are from.
In the grace of acceptance, our hearts learn to fly,
As echoes of love linger, never say goodbye.

Through the tapestry woven, with colors so bright,
We honor each chapter, each struggle, each light.
In the grace of fading, a promise we'll find,
In unity's grace, our spirits aligned.

So let us walk forward, with gratitude pure,
For in every ending, new beginnings endure.
In the grace of fading echoes, we find our true way,
As we cherish the moments of each passing day.

Unbinding the Ties of Earth

In the stillness of night, we release the weight,
Ties that once bound us, we gently abate.
With wings spread wide, our spirits will soar,
Unbinding the ties, we open the door.

Through valleys of doubt, we venture anew,
With courage as compass, our hearts will break through.
In the dance of the stars, we find our true worth,
Unbinding the ties of this earthly berth.

For in moments of silence, the light will appear,
As whispers of love erase every fear.
In the depth of our souls, we seek what is true,
Unbinding the ties, we embrace something new.

The treasures we carry are found deep inside,
In the warmth of connection, our spirits will glide.
With faith as our anchor, we search and we learn,
Unbinding the ties, we rise with each turn.

So let us be vessels, of peace and of grace,
As we journey together, this life we will trace.
Unbinding the ties, with love as our guide,
In the realm of the heart, we shall always abide.

Milton Keynes UK
Ingram Content Group UK Ltd.
UKHW020041271124
451585UK00012B/974

9 789916 897102